HMH | into Math™

Teacher Edition – Book 1

Unit 1 Ways to Add and Subtract

Module 1 Addition Strategies

Copyright © 2020 by Houghton Mifflin Harcourt Publishing Company

All rights reserved. No part of this work may be reproduced or transmitted in any form or by any means, electronic or mechanical, including photocopying or recording, or by any information storage or retrieval system, without the prior written permission of the copyright owner unless such copying is expressly permitted by federal copyright law. Requests for permission to make copies of any part of the work should be submitted through our Permissions website at https://customercare.hmhco.com/contactus/Permissions.html or mailed to Houghton Mifflin Harcourt Publishing Company, Attn: Intellectual Property Licensing, 9400 Southpark Center Loop, Orlando, Florida 32819-8647.

Common Core State Standards © Copyright 2010. National Governors Association Center for Best Practices and Council of Chief State School Officers. All rights reserved.

This product is not sponsored or endorsed by the Common Core State Standards Initiative of the National Governors Association Center for Best Practices and the Council of Chief State School Officers.

Excerpt from *Principles for the Design of Mathematics Curricula: Promoting Language and Content Development* by Jeff Zwiers, Jack Dieckmann, Sara Rutherford-Quach, Vinci Daro, Renae Skarin, Steven Weiss, and James Malamut. Stanford University Center for Assessment, Learning and Equity. Reprinted by permission of Stanford University Center for Assessment, Learning and Equity.

Currency and Coins Photos Courtesy of United States Mint, Bureau of Engraving and Houghton Mifflin Harcourt

Printed in the U.S.A.

ISBN 978-0-358-13195-3

2 3 4 5 6 7 8 9 10   0877   28 27 26 25 24 23 22 21 20

4500797783   C D E F G

Authors

Edward B. Burger, PhD, is a mathematician who is also the president of Southwestern University in Georgetown, Texas. He is a former Francis Christopher Oakley Third Century Professor of Mathematics at Williams College, and a former vice provost at Baylor University. He has authored or coauthored numerous articles, books, and video series; delivered many addresses and workshops throughout the world; and made many radio and television appearances. He has earned many national honors, including the Robert Foster Cherry Award for Great Teaching. In 2013, he was inducted as one of the first fellows of the American Mathematical Society.

Juli K. Dixon, PhD, is a professor of mathematics education at the University of Central Florida (UCF). She has taught mathematics in urban schools at the elementary, middle, secondary, and post-secondary levels. She is a prolific writer who has published books, textbooks, book chapters, and articles. A sought-after speaker, Dr. Dixon has delivered keynotes and other presentations throughout the United States. Key areas of focus are deepening teachers' content knowledge and communicating and justifying mathematical ideas. She is a past chair of the National Council of Teachers of Mathematics Student Explorations in Mathematics Editorial Panel and a member of the board of directors for the Association of Mathematics Teacher Educators. You can find her on social media at @TheStrokeOfLuck.

Timothy D. Kanold, PhD, is an award-winning international educator, author, and consultant. He is a former superintendent and director of mathematics and science at Adlai E. Stevenson High School District 125 in Lincolnshire, Illinois. He is a past president of the National Council of Supervisors of Mathematics (NCSM) and the Council for the Presidential Awardees of Mathematics (CPAM). He has served on several writing and leadership commissions for National Council of Teachers of Mathematics during the past two decades, including the *Teaching Performance Standards* task force. He presents motivational professional development seminars worldwide with a focus on developing professional learning communities (PLCs) to improve teaching, assessing, and learning of *all* students. He has recently authored nationally recognized articles, books, and textbooks for mathematics education and school leadership, including *What Principals Need to Know About Teaching and Learning Mathematics* and *HEART!: Fully Forming Your Professional Life as a Teacher and Leader.* You can find him on social media at @tkanold.

Matthew R. Larson, PhD, is a past president of the National Council of Teachers of Mathematics (NCTM). Prior to serving as president of NCTM, he was the K–12 mathematics curriculum specialist for Lincoln Public Schools (Nebraska) where he currently serves as associate superintendent for instruction. A prolific speaker and writer, he is the coauthor of more than a dozen professional books. He was a member of the writing teams for the major publications *Principles to Actions: Ensuring Mathematical Success for All* (2014) and *Catalyzing Change in High School Mathematics: Initiating Critical Conversations* (2018). Key areas of focus include access and equity and effective stakeholder communication. He has taught mathematics at the secondary and college levels and held an appointment as an honorary visiting associate professor at Teachers College, Columbia University. You can find him on social media at @mlarson_math.

Steven J. Leinwand is a principal research analyst at the American Institutes for Research (AIR) in Washington, DC, and has nearly 40 years in leadership positions in mathematics education. He is a past president of the National Council of Supervisors of Mathematics and served on the National Council of Teachers of Mathematics Board of Directors. He is the author of numerous articles, books, and textbooks and has made countless presentations with topics including student achievement, reasoning, effective assessment, and successful implementation of standards. You can find him on social media at @steve_leinwand.

Jennifer Lempp is an author and educational consultant. She also currently serves as a coordinator in Fairfax County Public Schools, Virginia. She has taught at the elementary and middle school levels and served as a math coach for many years. She is Nationally Board Certified in Early Adolescence Mathematics and has facilitated professional development at the local, state, and national level on math workshop as a model for differentiated mathematics instruction. You can find her on social media at @Lempp5.

Program Consultants

English Language Development Consultant

Harold Asturias is the director for the Center for Mathematics Excellence and Equity at the Lawrence Hall of Science, University of California. He specializes in connecting mathematics and English language development as well as equity in mathematics education.

Program Consultant

David Dockterman, EdD, operates at the intersection of research and practice. A member of the faculty at the Harvard Graduate School of Education, he provides expertise in curriculum development, adaptive learning, professional development, and growth mindset.

Blended Learning Consultant

Weston Kieschnick, ICLE Senior Fellow, a former teacher, principal, instructional development coordinator, and dean of education, Weston Kieschnick has driven change and improved student learning in multiple capacities throughout his educational career. Now, as an experienced instructional coach and senior fellow with ICLE, Kieschnick shares his expertise with teachers to transform learning through online and blended models.

STEM Consultants

Michael Despezio has authored many HMH instructional programs for science and mathematics. He has also authored numerous trade books and multimedia programs on various topics and hosted dozens of studio and location broadcasts for various organizations in the US and worldwide. Recently, he has been working with educators to provide strategies for implementing the Next Generation Science Standards.

Marjorie Frank An educator and linguist by training, a writer and poet by nature, Marjorie Frank has authored and designed a generation of instructional materials in all subject areas. Her other credits include authoring science issues of an award-winning children's magazine, writing game-based digital assessments, developing blended learning materials, and serving as instructional designer and coauthor of school-to-work software. She has also served on the adjunct faculty of Hunter, Manhattan, and Brooklyn Colleges.

Bernadine Okoro is a chemical engineer by training and a playwright, novelist, director, and actress by nature. Okoro went from working with patents and biotechnology to teaching in K–12 classrooms. She is a 12-year science educator, Albert Einstein Distinguished Fellow, original author of NGSS and a member of the Diversity and Equity Team. Okoro currently works as a STEM learning advocate and consultant.

Cary I. Sneider, PhD While studying astrophysics at Harvard, Cary Sneider volunteered to teach in an Upward Bound program and discovered his real calling as a science teacher. After teaching middle and high school science, he settled for nearly three decades at Lawrence Hall of Science in Berkeley, California, where he developed skills in curriculum development and teacher education. Over his career, Cary directed more than 20 federal, state, and foundation grant projects and was a writing team leader for the Next Generation Science Standards.

Math Solutions® Program Consultants

Deepa Bharath, MEd
Professional Learning Specialist
Math Solutions
Jupiter, Florida

Nicole Bridge, MEd
Professional Learning Specialist
Math Solutions
Attleboro, Massachusetts

Treve Brinkman
Director of Professional Learning
Math Solutions
Denver, Colorado

Lisa K. Bush, MEd
Sr. Director, Professional Development
Math Solutions
Glendale, Arizona

Carol Di Biase
Professional Learning Specialist
Math Solutions
Melbourne, Florida

Stephanie J. Elizondo, MEd
Professional Learning Specialist
Math Solutions
Ocala, Florida

Christine Esch, MEd
Professional Learning Specialist
Math Solutions
Phoenix, Arizona

Le'Vada Gray, MEd
Director of Professional Learning
Math Solutions
Country Club Hills, Illinois

Connie J. Horgan, MEd
Professional Learning Specialist
Math Solutions
Jerome, Idaho

Monica H. Kendall, EdD
Professional Learning Specialist
Math Solutions
Houston, Texas

Lori Ramsey, MEd
Professional Learning Specialist
Math Solutions
Justin, Texas

Lisa Rogers
Professional Learning Specialist
Math Solutions
Cape Coral, Florida

Derek Staves, EdD
Professional Learning Specialist
Math Solutions
Greeley, Colorado

Sheila Yates, MEd
Professional Learning Specialist
Math Solutions
Sioux Falls, South Dakota

Classroom Advisors

Abbey Len Bobbett
Laguna Elementary School
Scottsdale Unified School District
Scottsdale, Arizona

Rebecca Boden
Grant County Board of Education
Grant County Schools
Williamstown, Kentucky

Nicole Bunger
Centennial Elementary
Higley Unified School District
Gilbert, Arizona

Marsha Campbell
Murray Elementary
Hobbs Municipal Schools
Hobbs, New Mexico

Nichole Gard
Palmyra Elementary
Palmyra R-1 School District
Palmyra, Missouri

Dena Morosin
Shasta Elementary School
Klamath County School District
Klamath Falls, Oregon

Joanna O'Brien
Palmyra Elementary
Palmyra R-1 School District
Palmyra, Missouri

Nora Rowe
Peoria Traditional Elementary
Peoria Unified School District
Peoria, Arizona

Terri Trebilcock
Fairmount Elementary
Jefferson County Public Schools
Golden, Colorado

Module 1: Addition Strategies

Module 2: Subtraction Strategies

Module 3: Properties of Operations

Module 4: Apply the Addition and Subtraction Relationship

Musician [STEM]

- Ask children to describe the picture in their own words. Elicit that the picture shows a girl playing a musical instrument. Discuss children's prior knowledge of what a musician does.

- **Say:** *You may hear music when watching a television show, looking at a commercial, or visiting a carnival. You also hear music when listening to the radio or attending a concert. Do you sing or play an instrument? If so, you are a musician too!*

- Explain to children that music is an art form, but musical sounds can be explained by science. Some careers in music rely on knowledge of science and math.

STEM Task:

Divide children into pairs or groups. Have children place their hands on their throats as they hum a short tune. Ask children to pay attention to the vibrations they feel. Next, have one partner drum on the desk while the other children feel the vibrations. Give children the opportunity to discuss the vibrations they felt.

Elicit from children that they use hearing and touch when listening to music. They may also use sight when they make music.

Unit 1 Project Card Math Music

Use after Lesson 1.1.

Overview: Children use music to represent addition equations.

Materials: musical instruments, scissors, glue, paper, markers, connecting cubes

Assessing Child Performance: Children should use tools or draw a picture to represent a number pair, such as 6 + 4 = 10. Then they make musical noises to represent the addends. Answers will vary depending on the number pair chosen and the musical instruments used.

Unit
1
Ways to Add and Subtract

Musician

Musicians play musical instruments. Some musicians sing songs. They may perform alone or in groups. You can listen to recorded music on a radio, a computer, or a phone.

Do you like to listen to music? What is your favorite song?

Unit 1

STEM Task:

Talk with a partner. What senses do you use when you make or listen to music?

one   1

[STEM]
Unit
1

Math Music

Let's make math music! Show number pairs in a musical way.

1. Use objects or drawings to model the addition parts of a number.
2. Now play the parts. So for 5 + 3 = 8:
   - Clap 5 times.
   - Stomp your feet 3 times.

Did you hear 5 + 3 = 8?

Do it again with other number pairs.

Grade 1, Unit 1

HMH Math

Learning Mindset
Try Again Collects and Tries Multiple Strategies

Sometimes you cannot solve a problem with one try. When you try again, you may need to change the way you do things. Having more than one strategy helps you to solve more problems.

Reflect

Q When did you need to try more than one strategy to solve a problem?

Q How do you feel when you try a different strategy and it works?

2   two

© Houghton Mifflin Harcourt Publishing Company

Social-Emotional Learning
Learning Mindset

Try Again: Collects and Tries Multiple Strategies

The learning mindset focus for this unit is *try again*. Children may be easily discouraged by challenging problem situations. When children are unable to solve a problem the first time, they may assume that they are not capable of solving it and want to give up.

Children are more likely to try again when they are equipped with multiple strategies. In this lesson, children will learn many different strategies to add and subtract. Encourage children to try different strategies until they are successful with one. Give children opportunities to help one another and discuss the strategies that work best for them.

Understanding Mindset Beliefs

Describe a time you did not finish a task on your first attempt. Discuss your feelings about the experience and explain how trying again helped you become successful. Ask children to think of reasons people may not try again, and invite them to share their own experiences. If children identify situations in which they were afraid to try again because of a fear of harsh criticism or a feeling that others would not perceive them as smart, address these fears directly. Then discuss reasons people would try again when they could not complete a task on the first try.

Developing Growth Mindset Behaviors

Once children have identified beliefs that make it likely for someone to try again, have them identify behaviors and strategies that work for them. Connect real-life examples to examples that can be used in the classroom. Discuss how approaching a single problem using a different strategy is one way to try again. Explain that in this unit, children will learn multiple strategies to add and subtract. Ask children to remember to try different strategies when they approach a problem that they are unable to solve on the first try.

What to Watch For

Watch for children who stop working after one attempt. Have these children:

• try a new strategy

• identify where they need assistance

• ask a friend or teacher for help

Watch for children who unsuccessfully use the same strategy over and over. Have these children:

• identify the strategy they have used

• brainstorm additional strategies

• try at least one new strategy

• evaluate the effectiveness of different strategies

"Success consists of getting up just one more time than you fall."

—Oliver Goldman

ADDITION STRATEGIES

Introduce and Check for Readiness
- Module Opener
- Are You Ready?

data
checkpoint

Lesson 1—1 Day
Build Understanding

Represent Addition
Learning Objective: Solve addition word problems and represent addition in different ways, such as with objects, drawings, and equations.
Review Vocabulary: add
New Vocabulary: equation, is equal to (=), plus (+), sum

Lesson 2—2 Days
Connect Concepts and Skills

Count On
Learning Objective: Use counting on as a strategy to solve addition facts.
New Vocabulary: count on

Lesson 3—1 Day
Connect Concepts and Skills

Add 10 and More
Learning Objective: Use ten frames to find the sum of 10 and a number less than 10.

Lesson 4—2 Days
Connect Concepts and Skills

Make a 10 to Add
Learning Objective: Use the *make a ten* strategy to solve addition facts.
New Vocabulary: make a ten

Lesson 5—1 Day
Connect Concepts and Skills

Add Doubles
Learning Objective: Represent and solve doubles facts.
New Vocabulary: doubles

Lesson 6—1 Day
Connect Concepts and Skills

Use Known Sums to Add
Learning Objective: Use doubles facts to solve other addition facts.
Online Professional Learning Video

Lesson 7—2 Days
Apply and Practice

Choose a Strategy to Add
Learning Objective: Apply strategies such as making a ten, counting on, and using doubles to solve addition word problems.

Assessment
- Module 1 Test (Forms A and B)
- Unit 1 Performance Task after Module 4

data
checkpoint

See the entire scope and sequence in the Planning and Pacing Guide.

Build Understanding   Connect Concepts and Skills   Apply and Practice

TEACHING FOR DEPTH: Addition Strategies

Meaning of Counting On 1, 2, 3 The goal in teaching this strategy is to help children move from counting all in two groups to counting on from the larger group.

- Counting on is an efficient strategy for adding 1, 2, or 3, but an inefficient strategy when adding more than 3.
- The prolonged use of counting on prevents children from achieving mastery of basic addition facts. They will learn other addition strategies to use when counting on is inefficient.

Meaning of Make a Ten to Add The *make a ten* strategy is based on the concept of ten and the understanding that numbers from 11 to 20 can be expressed as ten and some more.

- This process illustrates the use of the Associative property of addition. The fact $9 + 6$ is thought of as $9 + (1 + 5)$, then as $(9 + 1) + 5$.
- Ten frames are the most effective tools for helping children conceptualize the *make a ten* strategy.

Meaning of Doubles Doubles facts are generally easy for children to remember. These facts then become useful to help children learn facts with sums that are 1 more than the doubles fact.

- For example, to find the sum of $6 + 7$ or $7 + 6$, children can think $6 + 6 = 12$. So, the sum of $6 + 7$ or $7 + 6$ is 1 more than 12, or 13.

Mathematical Progressions

Prior Learning	Current Development	Future Connections
Children:	**Children:**	**Children:**
• solved addition word problems within 10.	• use strategies to add within 20, including counting on, making a ten, and using known doubles facts.	• will use mental strategies to fluently add within 20.
• counted numbers in order, beginning from a given number.	• solve addition word problems within 20.	• will know all sums of two one-digit numbers by memory.
• used objects, drawings, and equations to represent ways to make 10.	• relate counting to addition.	• will use addition within 100 to solve one- and two-step word problems.
• represented addition within 10 using objects, drawings, and equations.	• represent addition facts and solve addition word problems using objects, drawings, and equations.	

TEACHER ⟷ TO TEACHER

From the Classroom

Use and connect mathematical representations. One of the things I want to find out about the children in my classroom at the beginning of the year is what mathematical representations they are familiar with. Have they used ten frames, number paths, rekenreks, or pictures of hands? I spend time each day with small groups using visual addition problems, asking children to share their solution strategies. I make notes of who is consistently counting by ones, who is counting on, and whether anyone is using number relationships.

In whole class discussions, I also start asking questions to encourage children to visualize quantities and make connections between representations. If we are talking about the number 12 for example,

I ask children to close their eyes and picture that number on a ten frame. I might ask, "How many ten frames do you need to show 12? How do you know? What would 12 look like with your fingers? What would you color on a 100 chart?"

After these different representations are sketched and children have justified how each one shows 12, I say something like, "Show me the 2 in each representation. Show me the 10 in each representation. Why is there a 10 and a 2 in each representation?"

Discussions like these help me learn about the children in my classroom and start introducing them to tools that we will use all year long.

By giving all children regular exposure to language routines in context, you will provide opportunities for children to **listen for,** and **speak, read,** and **write** about mathematical situations. You will also give children the opportunity to develop understanding of both mathematical language and concepts.

Using Language Routines to Develop Understanding

Use the Professional Learning Cards for the following routines to plan for effective instruction.

Three Reads   Lessons 1.1, 1.2, 1.3, 1.5, and 1.6

Children read a problem or the teacher reads the problem three times with a specific focus each time.

1st Read What is the problem about?
2nd Read What do each of the numbers describe?
3rd Read What math questions could you ask about the problem?

Stronger and Clearer Each Time   Lessons 1.3 and 1.6

Children write their reasoning about a problem, share that reasoning, explain it, listen to feedback, respond to feedback, and then refine their reasoning by writing again.

Compare and Connect   Lessons 1.1, 1.2, 1.4, and 1.5

Children listen to a partner's solution strategy, identify it, and then compare it to and contrast it with their own.

Critique, Correct, and Clarify   Lessons 1.6 and 1.7

Children correct the work in a flawed explanation, argument, or solution method; share with a partner; and refine the sample work.

Connecting Language to Addition Strategies

Watch for children's use of review and new terms listed below as they explain their reasoning and make connections with new concepts.

Linguistic Note

Many key phrases use familiar words in new combinations. For example, *count on* may be discernable as individual words, but English Language Learners may have trouble understanding this as a phrase. Eliciting prior knowledge is essential to discovering unfamiliar phrases that children will need to understand to be successful with the lesson.

Key Academic Vocabulary

Current Development • Review and New Vocabulary

add find the sum of two or more numbers; find how many in all

count on to count forward from a given number

doubles an addition fact that includes two of the same number, such as $5 + 5$

equation a numerical sentence that shows two quantities are equal

is equal to ($=$) is a number or amount that is the same as

make a ten a strategy that teaches children to isolate a ten first to help them add numbers whose sum is greater than ten

plus ($+$) put together with

sum a number obtained as a result of addition

Module 1 Addition Strategies

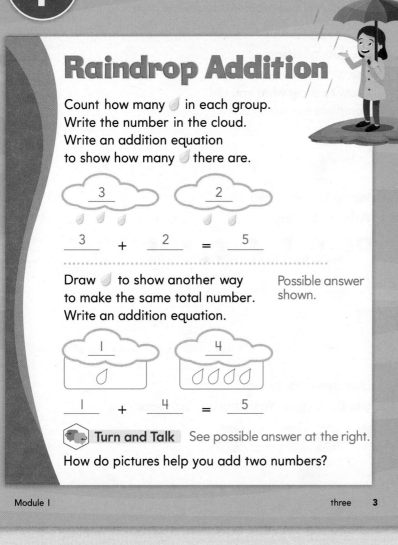

Raindrop Addition

Count how many 💧 in each group.
Write the number in the cloud.
Write an addition equation
to show how many 💧 there are.

3   2

3   +   2   =   5

Draw 💧 to show another way   Possible answer
to make the same total number.   shown.
Write an addition equation.

1   4

1   +   4   =   5

Turn and Talk   See possible answer at the right.

How do pictures help you add two numbers?

Module 1   three   **3**

COMMON ERRORS

Children may have difficulty listing both addends to find the total.

Watch for children who count only part of a visual model. For these children, point to each cloud at the top of the page. **Ask:**

• How many raindrops are there under each cloud?

Watch for children who cannot determine the relationship between the visual model and the addition equation. For these children, point to the equation. **Ask:**

• Use the number of raindrops under each cloud for the numbers you add. What numbers do you add?

• Use the number of raindrops under both clouds for the total. What number is the total?

Raindrop Addition

Assess Prerequisite Concepts
Grade K Module 6

Have children complete the Module Opener Task. This task can be used to determine understanding of the prerequisite concept *add within 5*.

Engage Children

Have children work in mixed-ability groups to complete the Module Opener Task. This task is designed to:

• activate prior knowledge that is essential for success in the upcoming module

• challenge children to think critically and justify their reasoning

• encourage cooperation, collaboration, and discourse within a group

Guide Children's Discussion

Listen for children who correctly use review vocabulary as part of their discourse. Children should be familiar with the terms *add* and *equation*. Ask children to explain what it means if they use those terms.

Sample Guided Discussion:

Q **What does the picture at the top of the page show you?** clouds and raindrops

Q **How could you use mathematics to describe the raindrops?** Possible answer: I could write an equation. The numbers I add show how many raindrops there are under each cloud.

Turn and Talk Encourage children to think about how the pictures on this page helped them to add. Possible answer: Pictures help me see how many are in each group. Then I can add the two numbers to find how many in all.

Extend the Task

• Have children draw their own visual model that shows another problem, such as $3 + 4 = 7$.

• Have children make a concrete model of the problem.

Assign the Digital Are You Ready? to power actionable reports including
- proficiency by standards
- item analysis

Are You Ready?

Diagnostic Assessment

- Diagnose prerequisite mastery.
- Identify intervention needs.
- Modify or set up leveled groups.

Have children complete the *Are You Ready?* assessment on their own. Items test the prerequisites required to succeed with the new learning in this module.

Model Addition This item will assess whether children can make concrete models to represent addition.

Write Numbers to 10 These items will assess whether children can write numerals to represent a given quantity up to 10.

Use Symbols to Add This item will assess whether children can use a visual model to write an addition equation.

Name _____

Are You Ready?

Complete these problems to review prior concepts and skills you will need for this module.

Model Addition

Use ● to show each number.
Draw to show what you did.
Complete the equation.

1 ◯   ◯ ◯
  1   2

$1 + 2 = \underline{3}$

Write Numbers to 10

Write how many.

2  _____ 6 ducks

3 ★★★★ ★★★★   _____ 8 stars

Use Symbols to Add

Use the picture. Write the addition equation.

4

$\underline{3} + \underline{1} = \underline{4}$

4   four

© Houghton Mifflin Harcourt Publishing Company

DATA-DRIVEN INTERVENTION

MTSS RtI

Concept/Skill	Objective	Prior Learning *	Intervene with
Model Addition	Represent addition using a concrete model and an equation.	Grade K, Lesson 5.3	• Tier 3 Skill 5 • Reteach, Grade K, Lesson 5.3
Write Numbers to 10	Write numbers up to 10.	Grade K, Lessons 8.1–8.3	• Tier 2 Skill 1 • Reteach, Grade K, Lessons 8.1–8.3
Use Symbols to Add	Write an addition equation.	Grade K, Lesson 11.5	• Tier 2 Skill 9 • Reteach, Grade K, Lesson 11.5

* Your digital materials include access to resources from Grades K–3. The lessons referenced here contain a variety of resources you can use with children who need support with this content.

1.1 Represent Addition

LESSON FOCUS AND COHERENCE

■ Major □ Supporting ○ Additional

Mathematics Standards
■ Use addition and subtraction within 20 to solve word problems involving situations of adding to, taking from, putting together, taking apart, and comparing, with unknowns in all positions, e.g., by using objects, drawings, and equations with a symbol for the unknown number to represent the problem.

Mathematical Practices and Processes (MP)
• Model with mathematics.
• Use appropriate tools strategically.

I Can Objective 🎧
I can represent addition using equations, pictures, and objects.

Learning Objective
Solve addition word problems and represent addition in different ways, such as with objects, drawings, and equations.

Language Objective
• Explain the meaning of terms and symbols: *add*, *equation*, *is equal to* (=), *plus* (+), and *sum*.

Vocabulary
Review: add

New: equation, is equal to (=), plus (+), sum

Lesson Materials: pencils, MathBoard, connecting cubes, two-color counters, crayons

Mathematical Progressions

Prior Learning	Current Development	Future Connections
Children: • solved addition word problems within 10. **(GrK, 11.3)** • represented addition within 10 using objects, drawings, and equations. **(GrK, 11.3, 11.5, 12.1, and 12.3)**	**Children:** • solve addition word problems within 20. • represent addition facts using objects, drawings, and equations.	**Children:** • will use addition within 100 to solve one- and two-step word problems. **(Gr2, 15.1 and 15.3)** • will represent addition within 100 using drawings and equations. **(Gr2, 14.3)**

UNPACKING MATH STANDARDS

Use addition and subtraction within 20 to solve word problems involving situations of adding to, taking from, putting together, taking apart, and comparing, with unknowns in all positions, e.g., by using objects, drawings, and equations with a symbol for the unknown number to represent the problem.

What It Means to You
Throughout Grade 1, children will solve a variety of word problems involving basic addition and subtraction facts and represent those problems in multiple ways. Concrete objects used by children include tools such as connecting cubes, counters, and ten frames. Pictorial representations may be simple illustrations of problems or more complex diagrams.

This lesson focuses on how these kinds of representations can be used for addition. In later lessons, children will explore these representations in more depth and apply them to various addition strategies and problem types. In Module 2, children will begin to explore ways to represent subtraction. Equations will include unknown numbers that may not be the sum or difference, such as $9 + \blacksquare = 16$ or $\blacksquare - 8 = 4$.

WARM-UP OPTIONS

ACTIVATE PRIOR KNOWLEDGE • Represent Addition

Use these activities to quickly assess and activate prior knowledge as needed.

Math Routine

Equal to What How many counters do you see?

Explain how you know how many there are.

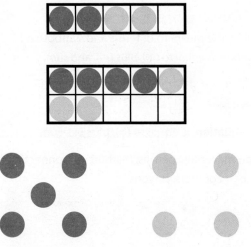

Reveal the top image (the five frame) for 2 to 3 seconds. Give children think-time before asking them to show a "thumbs-up" when they have an answer. Then invite volunteers to share their answers with the class. Ask children to say the number they saw and explain how they saw it. For example, one child may know there are 4 counters because there is 1 empty box in the five frame. Another child may see two groups of 2 counters or $2 + 2 = 4$. Another child may count each counter.

Repeat with the remaining two images. Encourage children to include addition in their responses if they do not already do so.

Make Connections

Based on children's responses to the Math Routine, choose one of the following:

1 Project the Interactive Reteach, Grade K, Lesson 11.3.

2 Complete the Prerequisite Skills Activity:

Have children make a concrete model of the problem with their counters as they act it out. *There are 4 cats.* Have 4 children stand, and the rest of the children show 4 counters. *3 more cats join them.* 3 children act this out, and the rest of the children use 3 counters. *How many cats are there now?* Make sure that children put the counters together, or add, to find the total number of cats. Discuss the addition equation that models the problem. $4 + 3 = 7$

If children continue to struggle, use Tier 3 Skill 5.

SHARPEN SKILLS

If time permits, use this on-level activity to build fluency and practice basic skills.

Fluency—Addition Within 10

Objective: Fluently add within 10.
Materials: two-color counters, Fluency Builder: Addition Level 1 (Differentiated Instruction Blackline Masters)

Have children work in pairs. Give each child 5 counters. Have each child put some or all of the counters under their hand, and slide them to the center of the table. On the count of 3, both children uncover their counters. Children write the sum of the 2 groups of counters. If each child gets the sum correct, they each get 1 point. If only one child gets the sum correct, that child gets 2 points. The first child to get to 5 points wins the round.

Children can then complete the Fluency Builder worksheet to practice addition within 10.

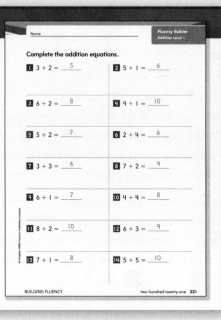

Represent Addition

(I Can) represent addition using equations, pictures, and objects.

Spark Your Learning

How can you use the number of big dogs and the number of little dogs to find how many dogs are in the picture?

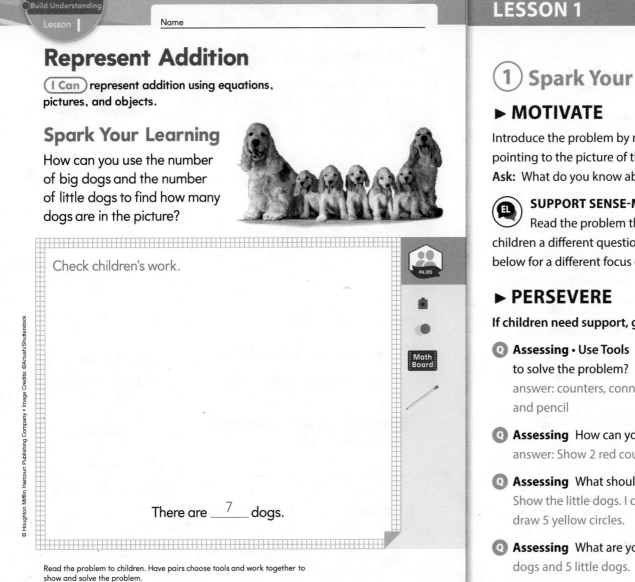

Check children's work.

There are ___7___ dogs.

Read the problem to children. Have pairs choose tools and work together to show and solve the problem.

Module 1 • Lesson 1   five   5

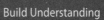

① Spark Your Learning

▶ MOTIVATE

Introduce the problem by reading it aloud to children and pointing to the picture of the dogs at the top of the page. **Ask:** What do you know about dogs?

SUPPORT SENSE-MAKING Three Reads
Read the problem three times for children. Ask children a different question shown in the Three Reads box below for a different focus each time.

▶ PERSEVERE

If children need support, guide them by asking:

Q Assessing • Use Tools Which tools could you use to solve the problem? Answers will vary. Possible answer: counters, connecting cubes, my fingers, paper and pencil

Q Assessing How can you show the big dogs? Possible answer: Show 2 red counters or draw 2 red circles.

Q Assessing What should you do next? Possible answer: Show the little dogs. I can show 5 yellow counters or draw 5 yellow circles.

Q Assessing What are you adding? I am adding 2 big dogs and 5 little dogs.

Q Advancing What addition fact shows how to combine those numbers? Possible answers: $2 + 5 = 7$, $5 + 2 = 7$, $7 = 2 + 5$, or $7 = 5 + 2$

Turn and Talk Ask children to explain how their drawings or concrete models show addition.
Possible answer: My drawing shows addition because I am adding a group of 2 and a group of 5 to show the total.

▶ BUILD SHARED UNDERSTANDING

Select children who have used various strategies and tools to share with the class how they solved the problem. Have children discuss why they chose a specific strategy or tool.

SUPPORT SENSE-MAKING • Three Reads

Read the problem stem three times and prompt the children with a different question each time.

1 What is the problem about?
There are big and little dogs.

2 What do each of the numbers describe?
One number describes how many big dogs are in the picture (2). Another number describes how many little dogs there are (5).

3 What math questions could you ask about the problem?
Possible questions: How many big dogs are there? How many little dogs are there? How many dogs are in the picture?

② Learn Together

Build Understanding

Task 1 (MP) **Model with Mathematics** When modeling a problem with an addition equation, it is important that children understand that the sum may appear before or after the equal sign. Make sure children understand that this problem could also be modeled with the equation $7 + 5 = 12$ (or $5 + 7 = 12$).

CONNECT TO VOCABULARY

Have children use the **Interactive Glossary** during this conversation to record their understanding.

EL **CONNECT MATH IDEAS, REASONING, AND LANGUAGE** **Compare and Connect**

Have children describe the meaning of **equation**, **is equal to (=)**, **plus (+)**, and **sum** in their own words. Have partners share their work and discuss how their descriptions compare and contrast.

Sample Guided Discussion:

Q **What tools can you use to represent the problem?**
Possible answer: connecting cubes or counters

Q **What does the word *sum* mean? What is the sum when you add 7 and 5?** the total when you add; 12

Turn and Talk Encourage children to share their work and discuss the symbols used in addition equations. Possible answer: It means *the same as*. So, the amount on the left is the same as the amount on the right.

Build Understanding

There are 7 blue fish and 5 yellow fish in a tank. How many fish are in the tank?

A How can you show the problem?

Possible answer shown.

B B B B B B B   Y Y Y Y Y

B How many blue fish are there? ___7___
How many yellow fish are there? ___5___

C How can you write an **equation** to find the sum?
___12___ = ___7___ + ___5___ Also accept $12 = 5 + 7$.

D There are ___12___ fish in the tank.

> **Connect to Vocabulary**
> 2 **plus** 1 **is equal to** 3.
> $2 + 1 = 3$
> The **sum** is 3.

Turn and Talk In an equation, what does the equal sign mean? See possible answer at the left.

LEVELED QUESTIONS

Depth of Knowledge (DOK)	Leveled Questions	What Does This Tell You?
Level 1 **Recall**	How can you use objects to show the problem? Possible answer: I can use connecting cubes to show the number of blue fish and yellow fish, and put the cubes together to show the total.	Children's answers to this question will demonstrate whether they understand how to represent addition using a concrete model.
Level 2 **Basic Application of Skills & Concepts**	How do you find the total number of fish? Possible answer: I can add the number of blue fish and the number of yellow fish.	Children's answers to this question will demonstrate whether they understand how to use addition to solve a problem.
Level 3 **Strategic Thinking & Complex Reasoning**	How can you model the problem with an equation? Possible answer: $12 = 7 + 5$	Children's answers to this question will demonstrate whether they understand how to model a problem with an addition equation.

There are 6 cats. 9 more cats join them.
How many cats are there now?

A How can you show the problem?

Possible answer shown.

● ● ● ● ● ● ○ ○ ○ ○ ○ ○ ○ ○ ○

B **Add.** Write an equation to solve.

____6____ + ____9____ = ____15____   Also accept 9 + 6 = 15.

C There are ____15____ cats now.

Check Understanding Math Board

Write an equation to solve.   Also accept 5 + 8 = 13.

1 Harry sees these animals.
How many animals does he see?

____8____ + ____5____ = ____13____

____13____ animals

Add. Write the sum.

2 6 + 3 = ____9____   3 7 + 7 = ____14____   4 ____6____ = 5 + 1

© Houghton Mifflin Harcourt Publishing Company

Task 2  **Use Tools** Children may use counters or connecting cubes to represent the problem. Encourage them to also draw a picture to illustrate their thinking.

Sample Guided Discussion:

Q **What numbers are you adding?** 6 and 9

Q **What do you get when you add the numbers?**
the total number of cats

Q **How do you model the problem with addition?**
Possible answer: I write an equation to show that the number of cats to start plus the number of cats that join is equal to the total number of cats now.

data checkpoint

---

③ Check Understanding

Formative Assessment

Use formative assessment to determine if your children are successful with this lesson's learning objective.

Children who successfully complete the Check Understanding can continue to the On Your Own practice.

For children who miss 1 problem or more, work in a pulled small group with the Tabletop Flipchart Mini-Lesson.

ONLINE **Ed** **Assign the Digital Check Understanding to determine**
• success with the learning objective
• items to review
• grouping and differentiation resources

④ Differentiation Options

Differentiate instruction for all children using small-group mini-lessons and math center activities on page 5C.

Reteach — Represent Addition

Challenge — Farm Scenes

Assign the Digital On Your Own for
• built-in student supports
• Actionable Item Reports
• Standards Analysis Reports

On Your Own

■ **Problem 5 • Model with Mathematics** Children write an addition equation to model and solve a word problem.

■ **Problem 6 • Open Ended** Children choose the numbers that will be added to make 16.

■ **Problems 7–12** Children solve addition facts.

⑤ Wrap-Up

Summarize learning with your class. Consider using the Exit Ticket, Put It in Writing, or I Can scale.

Exit Ticket

There are 4 elephants in the field.
Then 2 elephants join them.
What equation can you use to find
how many elephants there are now?
Possible answer: $4 + 2 = 6$

Put It in Writing

Explain when you would choose to model a problem with an addition equation.

I Can

The scale below can help you and your students understand their progress on a learning goal.

4	I can represent addition using equations, pictures, and objects and describe the steps used to solve the problem.
3	I can represent addition using equations, pictures, and objects.
2	I can act out addition.
1	I can represent amounts using numbers, pictures, and objects.

On Your Own

Write an equation to solve.

5 **MP Model with Mathematics**
Nathan has 2 cats. Larissa has 4 cats.
How many cats do they have?

$$\underline{2} + \underline{4} = \underline{6}$$

$\underline{6}$ **cats**   Also accept $4 + 2 = 6$.

6 **Open Ended** Paul and Rachel have a total of 16 stickers. Write an equation to show how many stickers Paul and Rachel could each have. Draw to show your thinking.
Accept any equation with a sum of 16.

$$\underline{16} = \underline{7} + \underline{9}$$

Check children's drawings.

Add. Write the sum.

7 $6 + 1 = \underline{7}$	**8** $2 + 8 = \underline{10}$	**9** $4 + 9 = \underline{13}$
10 $\underline{10} = 4 + 6$	**11** $\underline{8} = 3 + 5$	**12** $\underline{15} = 8 + 7$

⚙ I'm in a Learning Mindset!

Was I able to follow the directions?
What part of the directions were not clear?

_____

_____

Learning Mindset   mindset works

Try Again Learns Effectively

Ask children to think about the directions during this lesson. Encourage them to elaborate on the directions that helped them be successful. Ask children to describe the part of the directions that were not clear. *When you start something new, it is important to know what your goal is. Directions for these problems tell you your learning goal, and sometimes they also tell you how to get to your goal. It is important that the directions are clear to you. If they are not clear, read them again or ask someone to explain the directions in a different way. Sometimes you can figure out what you need to do by looking at the problem.*

Assignment Guide

Reference the chart below for problems associated with tasks. In a 2-day lesson, reference the chart to assign daily homework.

Learn Together Tasks	On Your Own Problems
Task 1, p. 6	Problems 6, 10, 11, and 12
Task 2, p. 7	Problems 5, 7, 8, and 9

ONLINE

Assign the Digital More Practice/
Homework for
• built-in student supports
• Actionable Item Reports
• Standards Analysis Reports

Name _____

LESSON 1.1
More Practice/
Homework

ONLINE
Video Tutorials and
Interactive Examples

Represent Addition

(MP) **Model with Mathematics**
Write an equation to solve.

1 Kelly eats 5 green grapes and 4 red grapes.
How many grapes does Kelly eat?

__5__ + __4__ = __9__   Also accept 4 + 5 = 9.

__9__ grapes

2 Kim puts 7 books on the table.
Then she puts 6 more books on the table.
How many books are on the table now?

__7__ + __6__ = __13__   Also accept 6 + 7 = 13.

__13__ books

3 **Open Ended** Jamal and Kim
have a total of 10 plants.
Write an equation to show
how many plants Jamal
and Kim could each have.
Draw to show your thinking.

> Accept any equation
> with a sum of 10.
> Check children's
> drawings.

__10__ = __7__ + __3__

Add. Write the sum.

4 7 + 7 = __14__   **5** 9 + 6 = __15__   **6** __9__ = 1 + 8

Module 1 • Lesson 1   one **P1**

© Houghton Mifflin Harcourt Publishing Company

More Practice/Homework

Represent Addition

Use More Practice/Homework pages to provide children
with additional practice applying the concepts and skills
presented in the lesson.

- **Problems 1 and 2 • Model with Mathematics** Children
  model an addition problem with an equation.

- **Problem 3 • Open Ended** Children solve an open-ended
  addition problem.

- **Problems 4–6** Children solve addition facts.

Assignment Guide

Reference the chart below for problems associated with tasks. In a 2-day lesson,
reference the chart to assign daily homework.

Learn Together Tasks	More Practice/Homework Problems
Task 1, p. 6	Problems 3, 6, 7, and 8
Task 2, p. 7	Problems 1, 2, 4, 5, 7, and 9

Test Prep

The Test Prep items provided assess understanding of representing addition and solving addition problems.

Additional Test Prep opportunities are available online and in *Getting Ready for High Stakes Assessments*.

Spiral Review

The spiral review problems will help determine if children have retained information taught in the past. Here, children will need to demonstrate the ability to count within 10. **(GrK, 7.5)**

Test Prep

Fill in the bubble next to the correct answer.

7 There are 8 ducks on the pond.
Then 5 more ducks fly to the pond.
How many ducks are there now?

○ 3 ducks

○ 12 ducks

● 13 ducks

8 1 tree is tall. 7 trees are short.
Which equation shows
how many trees there are?

○ $7 = 6 + 1$ ● $8 = 1 + 7$ ○ $9 = 1 + 8$

9 7 fish swim. 8 fish join them.
Which equation shows
how many fish swim now?

○ $7 + 1 = 8$ ● $7 + 8 = 15$ ○ $10 + 7 = 17$

Spiral Review

10 Count the number of ants.
Write the number.

<u> 6 </u>

ANCHOR-CHART OPTION

As you progress through the module, build and display an anchor chart.

EL CONNECT MATH IDEAS, REASONING, AND LANGUAGE Collect and Display

Have children build their own anchor chart in their Practice and Homework Journal.

A completed chart for the module is shown here.

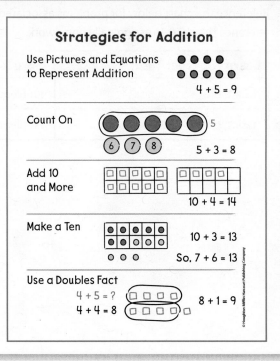

1.2 Count On

LESSON FOCUS AND COHERENCE

■ Major □ Supporting ○ Additional

Mathematics Standards
■ Relate counting to addition and subtraction (e.g., by counting on 2 to add 2).

Mathematical Practices and Processes (MP)
• Use appropriate tools strategically.

I Can Objective
I can count on to add.

Learning Objective
Use counting on as a strategy to solve addition facts.

Language Objectives
• Explain the meaning of *count on* in context.
• Describe how to count on to solve addition facts.

Vocabulary
New: count on

Lesson Materials: pencils, connecting cubes, two-color counters, MathBoard

Mathematical Progressions

Prior Learning	Current Development	Future Connections
Children: • counted numbers in order, beginning from a given number. **(GrK, 9.3)** • connected counting to cardinality. **(GrK, 7.5)**	**Children:** • relate counting to addition. • count on to add within 20.	**Children:** • will use mental strategies to fluently add within 20. **(Gr2, 1.2)** • will know all sums of two one-digit numbers from memory. **(G2, 1.2)**

UNPACKING MATH STANDARDS

Relate counting to addition and subtraction (e.g., by counting 2 to add 2).

What It Means to You
In this lesson, children learn that they may count on to add by using the greater addend as the starting point and adding on the second addend to find the total. For example, to add 3 + 9, children think: *Start with 9 and count on 3 more: 10, 11, 12. So, 3 + 9 = 12.* This strategy is often represented by using jumps on a number line, but some children may use their fingers, count on mentally, or use other tools. Counting on is an efficient addition strategy when one of the addends is 1, 2, or 3.

In the next module, children will learn that counting on can also be used as a strategy to solve subtraction problems (by counting on from the subtrahend until they reach the minuend).

ACTIVATE PRIOR KNOWLEDGE • Use Symbols to Add

Use these activities to quickly assess and activate prior knowledge as needed.

Math Routine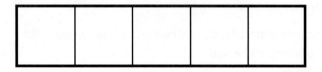

Number Talk

Show some counters inside the five frame.
Then, show some counters outside the five frame.
How can you use the plus symbol to show
how many counters there are in all?

Display the problem above and read it aloud. Have children solve the problem on their own. Children may show their thinking on their MathBoards. If available, provide five frames and counters.

Have volunteers share their drawings (or concrete models) and invite them to explain how they used the plus symbol. Encourage children to use mathematical language, such as *plus symbol, equal symbol, equation,* and *sum.* Accept all answers, including equations with the sum after the equal symbol, equations with the sum before the equal symbol, and equations with the addends in a different order. (Also accept addition in vertical form, although children are not expected to know how to do this yet.) Discuss how the ways to use the plus symbol are similar and how they are different.

Make Connections

Based on children's responses to the Math Routine, choose one of the following:

1 Project the Interactive Reteach, Grade K, Lesson 11.5.

2 Complete the Prerequisite Skills Activity:

Demonstrate how to use counters to represent the following problem:

I have 4 counters. I find 2 more counters.
How many counters do I have now?

Write out the equation as you place 4 red counters in front of children. For example, say, "Since I started with 4 counters, I will write 4 to start the equation." Add 2 yellow counters and write "+ 2" in the equation. Have children help you find the sum by counting all the counters. Complete the equation, including the = symbol.

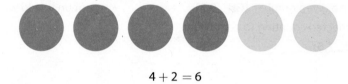

$$4 + 2 = 6$$

Repeat with other numbers of counters. Guide children through writing their own equations on their papers.

If children continue to struggle, use Tier 2 Skill 9.

SHARPEN SKILLS

If time permits, use this on-level activity to build fluency and practice basic skills.

Fluency—Addition Within 5

Objective: Fluently add within 5.

Have children complete the following addition facts without the use of paper and pencil.

$4 + 0 = \underline{\ 4\ }$ $2 + 1 = \underline{\ 3\ }$

$3 + 1 = \underline{\ 4\ }$ $2 + 2 = \underline{\ 4\ }$

$1 + 4 = \underline{\ 5\ }$ $3 + 2 = \underline{\ 5\ }$

Small-Group Options

Use these teacher-guided activities with pulled small groups at the teacher table.

On Track

Materials: two-color counters, connecting cubes, Number Line 0–12 (Teacher Resource Masters)

Have children demonstrate how to count on to add $7 + 3$. Allow them to use tools such as counters, connecting cubes, or a number line to illustrate their thinking.

Then repeat with $2 + 9$. Discuss whether it makes more sense to count on from 2 or from 9.

Almost There (RtI)

Materials: index cards

Use this Tabletop Flipchart Mini-Lesson to guide children as they count on to solve addition word problems and draw jumps on a number line to represent counting on to add.

Tabletop Flipchart:
Lesson 1.2

Mini-Lesson

Ready for More

Materials: chart paper, marker

Write a series of addition problems on chart paper:

$9 + 3 =$ ▪ $1 + 7 =$ ▪

$5 + 2 =$ ▪ $2 + 8 =$ ▪

Have the group work together to say a word problem that matches the first equation. Write their word problem on the chart paper. Then invite children to explain how to count on from the greater number to solve their word problem. Challenge children to demonstrate how to count on without the use of a concrete model.

Repeat the activity with the other equations as time allows.

Math Center Options

Use these student self-directed activities at centers or stations.   **Key:** ● Print Resources ● Online Resources

On Track

- ●● More Practice/Homework 1.2
- ● Interactive Glossary: **count on**
- ● Poggles MX: Addition and Subtraction, Level 15, Counting On
- ● Reader: *Join Us*

Almost There

- ● Reteach 1.2
- ● Interactive Reteach 1.2
- ● Game: 10 Ahead
- ●● RtI Tier 2 Skill 9: Use Symbols to Add

Ready for More

- ● Challenge 1.2
- ● Interactive Challenge 1.2

ONLINE ☺Ed   View data-driven grouping recommendations and assign differentiation resources.

During the *Spark Your Learning,* listen and watch for strategies students use. See samples of student work on this page.

Count On

Strategy 1

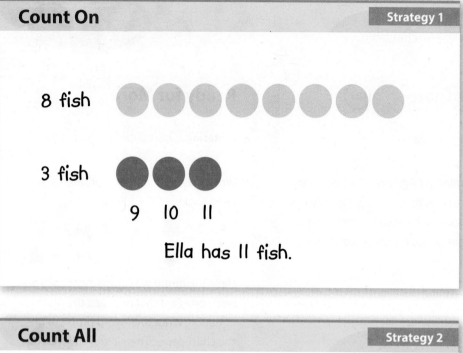

8 fish

3 fish

9 10 11

Ella has 11 fish.

If children . . . count on from the greater addend, they are demonstrating exemplary understanding of counting to solve an addition problem. (Some children may count on from 3. They will also get the correct answer, but the strategy is less efficient than counting on from 8.)

Have these children . . . share and explain how they counted on. **Ask:**

Q What strategy did you use to solve the problem?

Q How did you decide which number to start counting from?

Count All

Strategy 2

1 2 3 4 5 6 7 8 9 10 11

Ella has 11 fish.

If children . . . count each object or picture to find the total, they have successfully completed the task but they may not understand that there is a quicker way to solve the problem.

Activate prior knowledge . . . by showing children two sets of counters and having them consider how it is not necessary to count each one to find the total. **Ask:**

Q Look at this group of 8 yellow counters. If I add 3 red counters, do I need to count the yellow counters again to find how many there are in all? Explain.

COMMON ERROR: Miscounts

1 2 3 4 5 6 7 8 9 10

Ella has 10 fish.

If children . . . miscount their concrete or visual model, they may have difficulty counting objects precisely.

Then intervene . . . by encouraging children to keep track of each object as they count it. **Ask:**

Q If you have a row of counters, how can you keep track of them as you count?

Q Count your counters again. This time, carefully draw an X or write a number under each counter as you count it. How does that help you count?

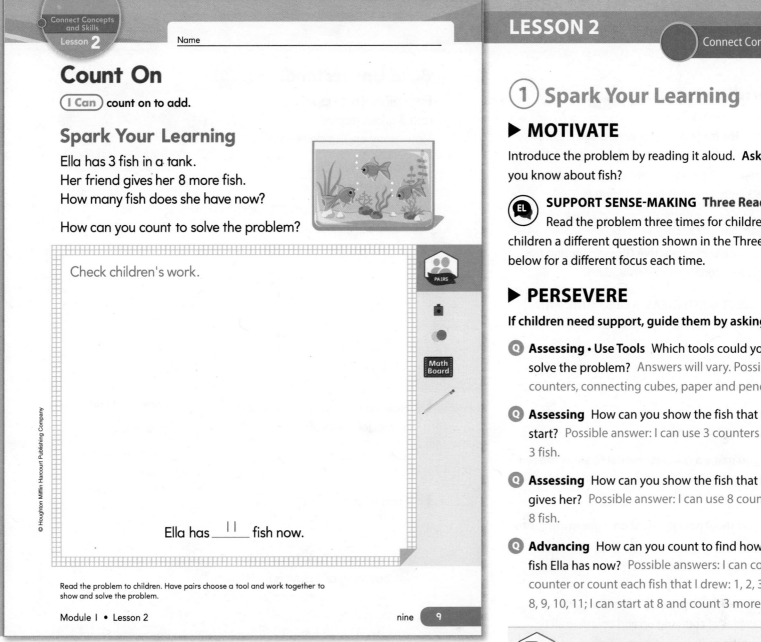

Name

Count On

(I Can) count on to add.

Spark Your Learning

Ella has 3 fish in a tank.
Her friend gives her 8 more fish.
How many fish does she have now?

How can you count to solve the problem?

Check children's work.

PAIRS

Math
Board

Ella has __|| __ fish now.

Read the problem to children. Have pairs choose a tool and work together to
show and solve the problem.

Module 1 • Lesson 2

nine **9**

---

(1) Spark Your Learning

▶ MOTIVATE

Introduce the problem by reading it aloud. **Ask:** What do
you know about fish?

(EL) **SUPPORT SENSE-MAKING Three Reads**
Read the problem three times for children. Ask
children a different question shown in the Three Reads box
below for a different focus each time.

▶ PERSEVERE

If children need support, guide them by asking:

Q **Assessing • Use Tools** Which tools could you use to
solve the problem? Answers will vary. Possible answer:
counters, connecting cubes, paper and pencil

Q **Assessing** How can you show the fish that Ella has to
start? Possible answer: I can use 3 counters or draw
3 fish.

Q **Assessing** How can you show the fish that Ella's friend
gives her? Possible answer: I can use 8 counters or draw
8 fish.

Q **Advancing** How can you count to find how many
fish Ella has now? Possible answers: I can count each
counter or count each fish that I drew: 1, 2, 3, 4, 5 , 6, 7,
8, 9, 10, 11; I can start at 8 and count 3 more: 9, 10, 11.

Turn and Talk What happens if you start at 8
and then count 3 more? Possible answer: I
count 9, 10, 11. That's the sum.

▶ BUILD SHARED UNDERSTANDING

Select children who have used various strategies and tools
to share with the class how they solved the problem. Have
children discuss why they chose a specific strategy or tool.

Read the problem stem three times and prompt the children with a different
question each time.

❶ What is the problem about?
Ella has some fish.

❷ What do each of the numbers describe?
She has 3 fish and gets 8 more.

❸ What math questions could you ask about the problem?
Possible questions: Do you need to add or subtract to solve?
How many fish does Ella have now?

② Learn Together

Build Understanding

Task 1 (**MP**) **Use Tools** In Part A, encourage children to first show the 9 red apples using a cube tower, a cube train, or a group of 9 counters. Then have them show how to count on 3 with 3 more cubes or counters.

CONNECT TO VOCABULARY

Have children use the **Interactive Glossary** during this conversation to record their understanding.

(**EL**) **CONNECT MATH IDEAS, REASONING, AND LANGUAGE** **Compare and Connect**

Have children describe the meaning of **count on** in their own words. Have partners share their work and discuss how their descriptions compare and contrast.

Sample Guided Discussion:

Q How can you make a concrete model to show the red apples? Possible answer: I can make a cube tower with 9 connecting cubes.

Q How can you show how to count on 3 green apples to solve? Possible answer: I can add 3 more cubes. I start at 9 and count on 3 more: 10, 11, 12.

Turn and Talk You may wish to provide examples of counting on and counting all to clarify the question. Possible answer: Both ways show you how to find the total number. Counting on is faster because you don't have to start counting from 1.

Build Understanding

Evan picks 9 red apples and 3 green apples. How many apples does he pick?

A How can you count on to solve the problem?

Possible answer shown.

B How can you write an equation to model the problem? Also accept $3 + 9 = 12$.

$$\underline{}9 + \underline{}3 = \underline{}12$$

C Evan picks ___12___ apples.

Connect to Vocabulary

count on

$4 + 2 = 6$
Say 4.
Count on 2 more.
5, 6

Turn and Talk How is counting on similar to counting all? How is it different? See possible answer at the left.

10 ten

LEVELED QUESTIONS

Depth of Knowledge (DOK)	Leveled Questions	What Does This Tell You?
Level 1 **Recall**	How can you make a concrete model that shows how many apples Evan picks? Possible answer: I can make a group of 9 counters and a group of 3 counters; that's 12 in all.	Children's answers to this question will demonstrate whether they can add to represent and solve the problem.
Level 2 **Basic Application of Skills & Concepts**	How can you add 9 and 3 using the *count on* strategy? Explain how to get to the sum. Possible answer: I can start at 9 and count on 3 more: 10, 11, 12. So, the sum is 12.	Children's answers to this question will demonstrate whether they can apply the *count on* strategy to arrive at the sum.
Level 3 **Strategic Thinking & Complex Reasoning**	How does the *count on* strategy help you add more quickly and more easily? Explain your thinking. Possible answer: The *count on* strategy allows me to start at the greater number without having to count from 1 to that number.	Children's answers to this question will demonstrate whether they can explain the purpose of the *count on* strategy and how it helps make addition more efficient.

Jade reads 2 books about cats and 5 books about dogs. How many books does she read?

A How can you count on to solve the problem?

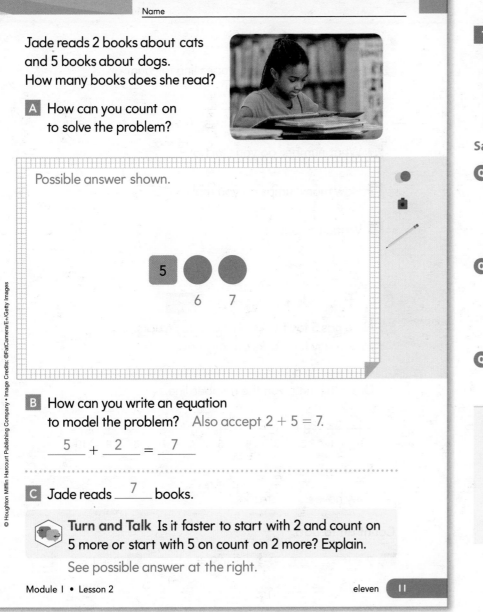

Possible answer shown.

| 5 | 6 | 7 |

B How can you write an equation to model the problem?   Also accept 2 + 5 = 7.

$$\underline{\quad 5 \quad} + \underline{\quad 2 \quad} = \underline{\quad 7 \quad}$$

C Jade reads ___7___ books.

Turn and Talk Is it faster to start with 2 and count on 5 more or start with 5 on count on 2 more? Explain.

See possible answer at the right.

Task 2 (MP) **Use Tools** Point out that the number 5 is already shown in the workspace, so children do not need to represent the 5 books about dogs with counters or connecting cubes. They only need to represent the 2 books about cats.

Sample Guided Discussion:

Q When you count on, it is faster to start with the greater number and count on from there. Look at the numbers you are adding in this problem. Which number is greater? 5

Q How can you make a concrete model to show how to count on? Possible answer: I start with the number 5 in the blue box. Then I add 2 counters to show counting on 2 more.

Q Say the numbers as you count on. What numbers do you say? First I say 5. Then I count on 2. So, I say 6, 7.

Turn and Talk Children should consider starting with each number. They should see that they arrive at the sum either way. Possible answer: It is faster to start with 5 and count on 2 more. Then I only need to count two numbers: 6, 7. If I start with 2, then I have to count a lot more numbers.

Step It Out

Task 3 (MP) **Use Tools** Introduce the number line to children and point out that the numbers shown are in the same order that they say when they are counting. Explain how a number line can be used as a tool for counting on.

Sample Guided Discussion:

Q What number will you start at when counting on? 7
(the greater number)

Q How can you show counting on 3 using the number line? Possible answer: I can draw 3 jumps from 7 to 10.

Q Why did you start at 7 and not 3? Possible answer: It is fewer jumps to start at 7 and it is quicker.

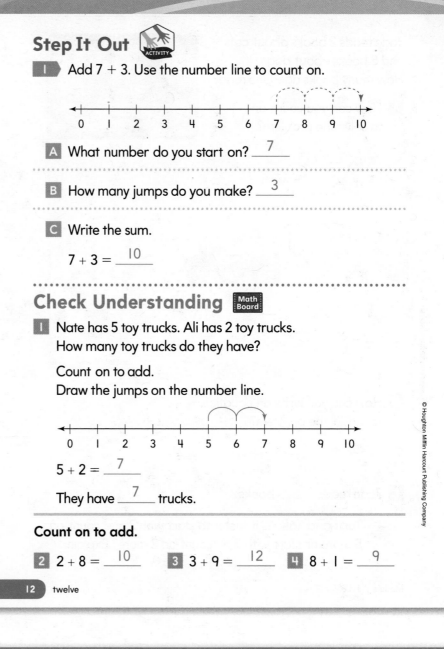

Step It Out

I   Add 7 + 3. Use the number line to count on.

A   What number do you start on? ___7___

B   How many jumps do you make? ___3___

C   Write the sum.

7 + 3 = ___10___

Check Understanding [Math Board]

I   Nate has 5 toy trucks. Ali has 2 toy trucks. How many toy trucks do they have?

Count on to add.
Draw the jumps on the number line.

5 + 2 = ___7___

They have ___7___ trucks.

Count on to add.

2   2 + 8 = ___10___   3   3 + 9 = ___12___   4   8 + 1 = ___9___

data checkpoint

③ Check Understanding

Formative Assessment

Use formative assessment to determine if your children are successful with this lesson's learning objective.

Children who successfully complete the Check Understanding can continue to the On Your Own practice.

For children who miss 1 problem or more, work in a pulled small group with the Tabletop Flipchart Mini-Lesson.

ONLINE :Ed

Assign the Digital Check Understanding to determine
• success with the learning objective
• items to review
• grouping and differentiation resources

④ Differentiation Options

Differentiate instruction for all children using small-group mini-lessons and math center activities on page 9C.

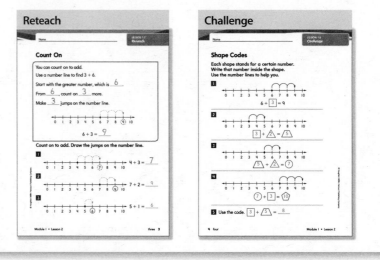

ONLINE

Assign the Digital On Your Own for
- built-in student supports
- Actionable Item Reports
- Standards Analysis Reports

Name _____

On Your Own

Count on to add.

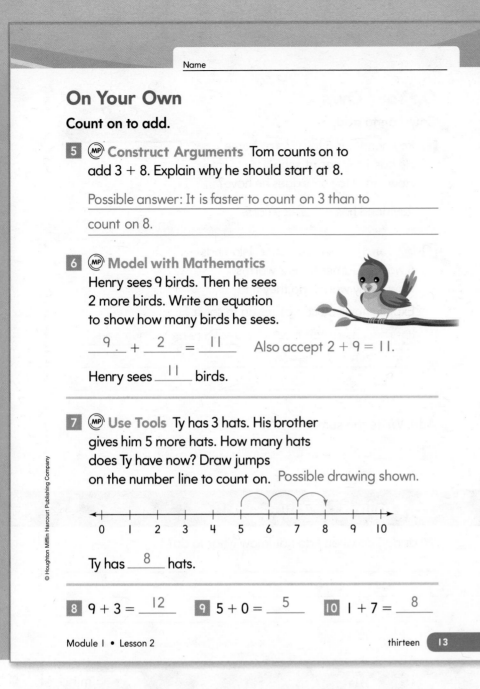

5 (MP) **Construct Arguments** Tom counts on to add 3 + 8. Explain why he should start at 8.

Possible answer: It is faster to count on 3 than to count on 8.

6 (MP) **Model with Mathematics**
Henry sees 9 birds. Then he sees 2 more birds. Write an equation to show how many birds he sees.

__9__ + __2__ = __11__   Also accept 2 + 9 = 11.

Henry sees __11__ birds.

7 (MP) **Use Tools** Ty has 3 hats. His brother gives him 5 more hats. How many hats does Ty have now? Draw jumps on the number line to count on. Possible drawing shown.

0 1 2 3 4 5 6 7 8 9 10

Ty has __8__ hats.

8 9 + 3 = __12__   **9** 5 + 0 = __5__   **10** 1 + 7 = __8__

Module 1 • Lesson 2   thirteen   **13**

© Houghton Mifflin Harcourt Publishing Company

On Your Own

- **Problem 5 • Construct Arguments** Children explain why they should count on from the greater number to add.

- **Problem 6 • Model with Mathematics** Children write an equation and count on to solve an addition problem.

- **Problem 7 • Use Tools** Children use a number line to solve an addition word problem.

- **Problems 8–10** Children count on to find the sum of addition facts. For Problem 9, remind children that adding 0 to a number does not change that number.

Assignment Guide

Reference the chart below for problems associated with tasks. In a 2-day lesson, reference the chart to assign daily homework.

Learn Together Tasks	On Your Own Problems
Task 1, p. 10	Problems 6, 11, and 12
Task 2, p. 11	Problems 5, 6, 11, and 12
Task 3, p. 12	Problems 7, 8, 9, 10, 13, 14, and 15

On Your Own

- **Problem 11** Children count on to solve an addition word problem.

- **Problem 12 · Construct Arguments** Children count on to solve an addition word problem and explain how they solved it.

- **Problems 13–15** Children count on to solve addition facts.

⑤ Wrap-Up

Summarize learning with your class. Consider using the Exit Ticket, Put It in Writing, or I Can scale.

Exit Ticket

Count on to add. What is 2 + 6? 8

Put It in Writing

Draw a picture that shows how you can add 8 + 3 by counting on. Use words to explain what the picture means.

I Can

The scale below can help you and your students understand their progress on a learning goal.

4	I can explain how to count on and why it can make adding quicker.
3	I can count on to add.
2	I can count on to add with the help of objects or pictures.
1	I can count all to add.

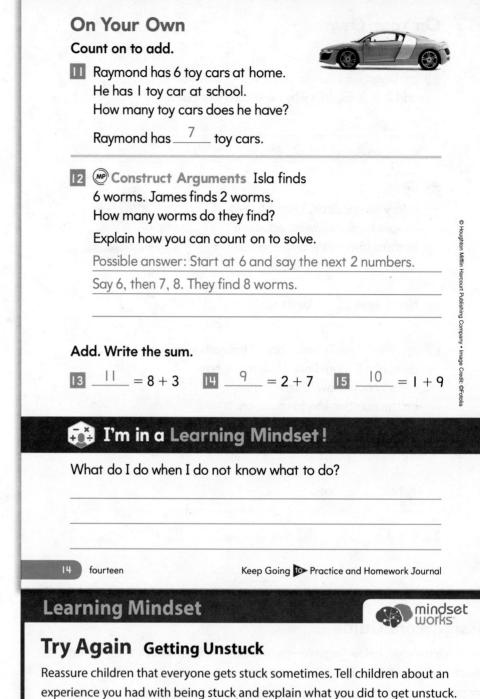

On Your Own

Count on to add.

11 Raymond has 6 toy cars at home.
He has 1 toy car at school.
How many toy cars does he have?

Raymond has ___7___ toy cars.

12 (MP) **Construct Arguments** Isla finds 6 worms. James finds 2 worms.
How many worms do they find?

Explain how you can count on to solve.

Possible answer: Start at 6 and say the next 2 numbers.

Say 6, then 7, 8. They find 8 worms.

Add. Write the sum.

13 __11__ = 8 + 3   **14** __9__ = 2 + 7   **15** __10__ = 1 + 9

⚙ I'm in a Learning Mindset!

What do I do when I do not know what to do?

_____

_____

_____

Learning Mindset

Try Again Getting Unstuck

Reassure children that everyone gets stuck sometimes. Tell children about an experience you had with being stuck and explain what you did to get unstuck.

When you get stuck on a problem, sometimes it is hard to know what to do to become unstuck. One way to get unstuck is to talk with someone else. Because there is more than one way to solve a problem, you may start to think about the problem in a different way.

Name _____

Count On

Count on to add.

1 (MP) **Construct Arguments**

Jody counts on to solve 1 + 7.
Explain why Jody should start at 7.

Possible answer: Counting on 1 from 7 is

faster than counting on 7 from 1.

2 (MP) **Model with Mathematics**

Ian has 6 small carrots and 3 big carrots.
Write an equation to show
how many carrots he has.

$\underline{6} + \underline{3} = \underline{9}$ Also accept 3 + 6 = 9.

Ian has $\underline{9}$ carrots.

3 **Math on the Spot** Which three numbers
can you use to complete the equation?

| 8 | 2 |
| 6 | 9 |

Jennifer has ▮ stamps.
She gets ▮ more stamps.
How many stamps does she have now?

$\underline{6} + \underline{2} = \underline{8}$ Also accept 2 + 6 = 8.

Jennifer has $\underline{8}$ stamps now.

4 9 + 1 = $\underline{10}$ **5** 5 + 2 = $\underline{7}$ **6** $\underline{11}$ = 3 + 8

Ed

Assign the Digital More Practice/ Homework for

- built-in student supports
- Actionable Item Reports
- Standards Analysis Reports

More Practice/Homework

Count On

Use More Practice/Homework pages to provide children with additional practice applying the concepts and skills presented in the lesson.

- **Problem 1 • Construct Arguments** Children explain why it makes sense to count on from the greater number.

- **Problem 2 • Model with Mathematics** Children write an equation and count on to solve a word problem.

- **Problems 4–6** Children count on to solve addition facts.

Math on the Spot

Math on the Spot

Encourage children to complete Problem 3 and then review their work with a family member or friend by watching the *Math on the Spot* video.

Assignment Guide

Reference the chart below for problems associated with tasks. In a 2-day lesson, reference the chart to assign daily homework.

Learn Together Tasks	More Practice/Homework Problems
Task 1, p. 10	Problems 2, 3, 8, and 9
Task 2, p. 11	Problems 1, 2, 3, 8, and 9
Task 3, p. 12	Problems 4–7

Test Prep

The Test Prep items provided assess understanding of adding by counting on.

Additional Test Prep opportunities are available online and in *Getting Ready for High Stakes Assessments.*

Spiral Review

The spiral review problems will help determine if children have retained information taught in the past. Here, children will need to demonstrate the ability to represent addition using an equation. **(1.1)**

Test Prep

Fill in the bubble next to the correct answer.

7 Count on to solve.
Which is the sum of $9 + 3$?

● 12 　　 ○ 11 　　 ○ 6

8 There are 2 frogs on a lily pad.
Then 7 more frogs join them.
How many frogs are on the lily pad now?
Count on to solve.

○ 8 frogs 　　 ● 9 frogs 　　 ○ 10 frogs

9 There are 8 birds in a tree.
1 bird is in a bush.
How many birds are there?
Count on to solve.

○ 7 birds 　　 ○ 8 birds 　　 ● 9 birds

Spiral Review

Write an equation to solve.

10 Lana holds 4 coins in one hand
and 6 coins in her other hand.
How many coins does she hold?

_4_ + _6_ = _10_ Also accept $6 + 4 = 10$.

_10_ coins

1.3 Add 10 and More

LESSON FOCUS AND COHERENCE

■ Major ☐ Supporting ○ Additional

Mathematics Standards

■ Add and subtract within 20, demonstrating fluency for addition and subtraction within 10. Use strategies such as counting on; making ten (e.g., $8 + 6 = 8 + 2 + 4 = 10 + 4 = 14$); decomposing a number leading to a ten (e.g., $13 - 4 = 13 - 3 - 1 = 10 - 1 = 9$); using the relationship between addition and subtraction (e.g., knowing that $8 + 4 = 12$, one knows $12 - 8 = 4$); and creating equivalent but easier or known sums (e.g., adding $6 + 7$ by creating the known equivalent $6 + 6 + 1 = 12 + 1 = 13$).

Mathematical Practices and Processes (MP)

- Use appropriate tools strategically.
- Look for and make use of structure.

I Can Objective

I can find the sum of 10 and some more.

Learning Objective

Use ten frames to find the sum of 10 and a number less than 10.

Language Objective

- Describe how to use ten frames to find sums.

Lesson Materials: Ten Frames (Teacher Resource Masters), pencils, two-color counters, connecting cubes

Mathematical Progressions

Prior Learning	Current Development	Future Connections
Children: • used objects, drawings, and equations to represent ways to make 10. **(GrK, 7.4)**	**Children:** • use strategies to add 10 and some more. • use counters and ten frames to represent addition of 10 and a one-digit addend.	**Children:** • will use the *make a ten* strategy to add within 20. **(Gr2, 1.5)** • will use mental strategies to fluently add within 20. **(Gr2, 1.2)** • will know all sums of two one-digit numbers from memory. **(Gr2, 1.2)**

UNPACKING MATH STANDARDS

Add and subtract within 20, demonstrating fluency for addition and subtraction within 10. Use strategies such as counting on; making ten (e.g., $8 + 6 = 8 + 2 + 4 = 10 + 4 = 14$); decomposing a number leading to a ten (e.g., $13 - 4 = 13 - 3 - 1 = 10 - 1 = 9$); using the relationship between addition and subtraction (e.g., knowing that $8 + 4 = 12$, one knows $12 - 8 = 4$); and creating equivalent but easier or known sums (e.g., adding $6 + 7$ by creating the known equivalent $6 + 6 + 1 = 12 + 1 = 13$).

What It Means to You

In this module, children explore addition strategies for adding numbers with sums to 20. In this lesson, children add 10 and a one-digit number. They use counters and ten frames as a concrete model to illustrate the strategy. Adding 10 and more lays the groundwork for the *make a ten* addition strategy, which is introduced in the next lesson. Other addition strategies in this module include counting on and using known sums (doubles) to add. In later modules, children will also explore subtraction strategies within 20 and the relationship between addition and subtraction.

WARM-UP OPTIONS

ACTIVATE PRIOR KNOWLEDGE • Make 10

Use these activities to quickly assess and activate prior knowledge as needed.

Math Routine

Building Numbers

Which pairs of ten frames show 10 counters?
Which pairs of ten frames do not show 10 counters?
Explain how you know.

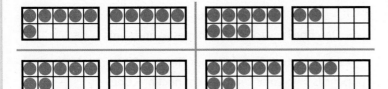

Reveal the first pair of ten frames. Give children think-time before asking them to show a "thumbs-up" if the ten frames show 10 counters in all or a "thumbs-down" if the ten frames do not. Have children support their conclusions, selecting children who have correctly and incorrectly interpreted the ten frames. If any children used equations, invite them to share their thinking. Encourage the other children to ask questions and critique each explanation.

Repeat with the other pairs of ten frames. For each pair of ten frames that does not show 10 counters, ask children how they could change the image to make it show 10 counters.

Make Connections

Based on children's responses to the Math Routine, choose one of the following:

1 Project the Interactive Reteach, Grade K, Lesson 7.4.

2 Complete the Prerequisite Skills Activity:

Have children use some red connecting cubes and some blue connecting cubes to make a cube train that is exactly 10 cubes long. Point out that are 10 cubes in all, so each cube train represents a way to make a 10.

Invite children to share and discuss their cube trains and their ways to make 10. Encourage them to name the addition fact that matches each cube train.

If children continue to struggle, use Tier 2 Skill 15.

SHARPEN SKILLS

If time permits, use this on-level activity to build fluency and practice basic skills.

Vocabulary Review

Objective: Build vocabulary fluency.

Write the word *ones* on the board. Invite children to tell what they know about counting by ones. Write the numbers 1 to 10 on the board and invite children to count by ones from 10. Stop when children reach the number 20.

Explain that counting by ones from 10 will help them with the addition strategy that they will learn in this lesson.

PLAN FOR DIFFERENTIATED INSTRUCTION

MTSS **RtI**

Small-Group Options
Use these teacher-guided activities with pulled small groups at the teacher table.

On Track

Materials: Ten Frames (Teacher Resource Masters), two-color counters

Display the equation $10 + 4 = \blacksquare$ and two ten frames. Represent the equation by placing 10 counters in the first ten frame and 4 counters in the second ten frame. Think aloud to demonstrate how to count from 10 to find the sum.

Then have children use the ten frames to represent $10 + 6 = \blacksquare$. Invite them to show how to find the sum by counting from 10.

Almost There (RtI)

Materials: Ten Frames (Teacher Resource Masters), two-color counters

Use this Tabletop Flipchart Mini-Lesson to guide children as they use ten frames to represent addition problems involving 10 and a one-digit addend.

Tabletop Flipchart:
Lesson 1.3

Mini-Lesson

Ready for More

Materials: chart paper, marker

On chart paper, prepare a horizontal number line (0–20) and a vertical number line (0–20).

Display the equation $10 + 3 = \blacksquare$. Building on children's experience with using ten frames to add 10 and more, demonstrate how the horizontal number line can be used to solve similar problems. Circle the number 10 on the number line and draw jumps to 11, 12, and 13. Circle 13 as the sum. Then repeat the activity using $10 + 5$ and the vertical number line, allowing children to guide each other through the steps.

Math Center Options
Use these student self-directed activities at centers or stations.   **Key:** ● **Print Resources** ● **Online Resources**

On Track

- ●● More Practice/Homework 1.3
- ● Fluency Maintenance: Addition
- ● Poggles MX: Addition and Subtraction, Level 28, Teen Addition

Almost There

- ● Reteach 1.3
- ● Interactive Reteach 1.3
- ● Game: 10 Ahead
- ●● RtI Tier 2 Skill 15: Make Groups of 10

Ready for More

- ● Challenge 1.3
- ● Interactive Challenge 1.3

ONLINE 🙂 **Ed**   View data-driven grouping recommendations and assign differentiation resources.

During the *Spark Your Learning,* listen and watch for strategies students use. See samples of student work on this page.

Count More from 10

Strategy 1

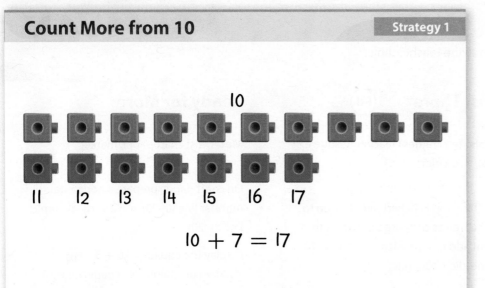

$$10 + 7 = 17$$

If children . . . count more from 10 to solve, they are demonstrating exemplary understanding of how to find the sum of 10 and more.

Have these children . . . share and explain how they represented and solved the problem. **Ask:**

Q What steps did you follow to find the number of shells in the pail now?

Q How did the group of 10 help you add?

Count All

Strategy 2

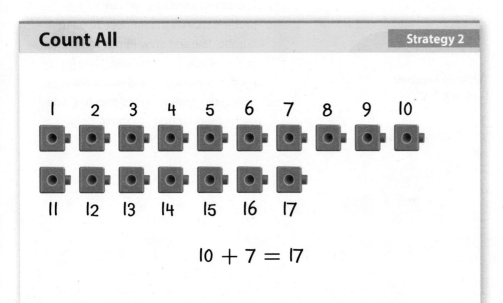

$$10 + 7 = 17$$

If children . . . solve the problem by counting each object in their concrete model, they may not understand that there are more efficient strategies they can use to add.

Activate prior knowledge . . . by encouraging children to count from 10. **Ask:**

Q What two numbers did you show in your concrete model?

Q How can you change your concrete model to show a group of 10 and some more?

Q How can you count from 10 to find the sum?

COMMON ERROR: Uses 10 as the Sum

$$7 + 3 = 10$$

If children . . . write an equation with 10 as the sum instead of an addend, they may not understand how to interpret the word problem.

Then intervene . . . by reminding children to think about the words that can help them recognize whether a given number is the sum. **Ask:**

Q How can you tell the word problem using your own words?

Q Is the number 10 a sum or one of the numbers that you are adding? What about the number 7? How do you know?

Add 10 and More

(I Can) find the sum of 10 and some more.

Spark Your Learning

Katie has 10 shells in a pail.
Then she puts 7 more shells into the pail.
How many shells are in the pail now?

How can you solve the problem?

Check children's work.

PAIRS

Math Board

There are ___17___ shells in the pail now.

Read the problem to children. Have pairs choose tools and work together to show and solve the problem. Then have children draw to show their work.

Module 1 • Lesson 3   fifteen **15**

© Houghton Mifflin Harcourt Publishing Company • Image Credit: ©Houghton Mifflin Harcourt

① Spark Your Learning

▶ MOTIVATE

Introduce the problem by reading it aloud. **Ask:** What do you know about shells?

EL **SUPPORT SENSE-MAKING Three Reads**
Read the problem three times for children. Ask children a different question shown in the Three Reads box below for a different focus each time.

▶ PERSEVERE

If children need support, guide them by asking:

Q **Assessing • Use Tools** How can you represent the problem? Possible answer: I can show 10 counters and 7 more counters.

Q **Advancing** How can you show this problem using an equation? Possible answers: $10 + 7 = 17$, $7 + 10 = 17$, $17 = 10 + 7$, $17 = 7 + 10$

Turn and Talk Look at your concrete model or picture. How can you use a group of 10 to help find how many there are in all? Possible answer: I can make a group of 10 counters and then use the other counters to count 7 more: 11, 12, 13, 14, 15, 16, 17.

EL **CULTIVATE CONVERSATION**
Stronger and Clearer

Have children share their Turn and Talk responses. Remind them to ask questions of each other that focus on how using a group of 10 can help them find the total. Then, have children refine their answers.

▶ BUILD SHARED UNDERSTANDING

Select children who have used various strategies and tools to share with the class how they solved the problem. Have children discuss why they chose a specific strategy or tool.

EL **SUPPORT SENSE-MAKING • Three Reads**

Read the problem stem three times and prompt the children with a different question each time.

❶ What is the problem about?
Katie has some shells.

❷ What do each of the numbers describe?
Katie has 10 shells in a pail. Then she puts 7 more in the pail.

❸ What math questions could you ask about the problem?
Possible questions: How many shells did she start with? How many more shells does she put in the pail? How can you write an addition equation to show this problem?

② Learn Together

Build Understanding

Task 1 (MP) **Use Tools** A set of two frames is a tool that children can use to show how to add 10 and a one-digit number. Children fill the first ten frame (to show 10) and part of the other ten frame (to show the one-digit addend). The two ten frames together represent the sum. Encourage children to also think of other tools that can be used to add 10 and a one-digit number. Discuss which tool works best for them.

Sample Guided Discussion:

Q **How can you use one of the ten frames to represent 10?**
Possible answer: I can place 1 counter in each box to represent each of the 10 ones.

Q **How can you use the other ten frame to represent 3?**
Possible answer: I can place 3 counters in the first 3 boxes.

Q **How can you use pictures to represent the same two numbers?** Possible answer: I can draw 10 red circles in one ten frame and 3 yellow circles in the other.

> **Turn and Talk** Encourage children to think about how the structure of the ten frames helps them to visualize the problem. Possible answer: I see the first ten frame is full, so I can start at 10 and then count on 3.

Build Understanding

Elena makes 10 bracelets.
Robin makes 3 bracelets.
How many bracelets do they make?

A How can you use the ten frames to show the problem?

Possible answer shown.

B How can you write an equation to solve the problem?

$$\underline{\hspace{0.3em}10\hspace{0.3em}} + \underline{\hspace{0.3em}3\hspace{0.3em}} = \underline{\hspace{0.3em}13\hspace{0.3em}}$$

C They make ___13___ bracelets.

> **Turn and Talk** How do the ten frames help you solve the problem? See possible answer at the left.

LEVELED QUESTIONS

Depth of Knowledge (DOK)	Leveled Questions	What Does This Tell You?
Level 1 **Recall**	What equation can help you solve this problem? Possible answer: $10 + 3 = 13$	Children's answers to this question will demonstrate whether they can write an equation to represent addition of 10 and a one-digit number.
Level 2 **Basic Application of Skills & Concepts**	How do the ten frames help you find the sum? Possible answer: I have 10 in one ten frame. I use the counters in the other ten frame to count more: 11, 12, 13.	Children's answers to this question will demonstrate whether they can use a concrete model to add 10 and a one-digit number.
Level 3 **Strategic Thinking & Complex Reasoning**	Abby and Hugo each use counters to find the sum of $10 + 3$. Abby uses ten frames with her counters. Hugo does not use ten frames with his counters. Who do you think will find the sum quicker? Explain. Possible answer: Abby will find the sum quicker because she can see that one of her ten frames is full. She can just count on 3 more from 10.	Children's answers to this question will demonstrate whether they can select the most efficient way of solving an addition problem and explain their reasoning for choosing a particular strategy.

Name _____

Step It Out

1 Hank catches 10 fish.
His uncle catches 6 fish.
How many fish do they catch?

A Use ⬤. Draw to show the fish.

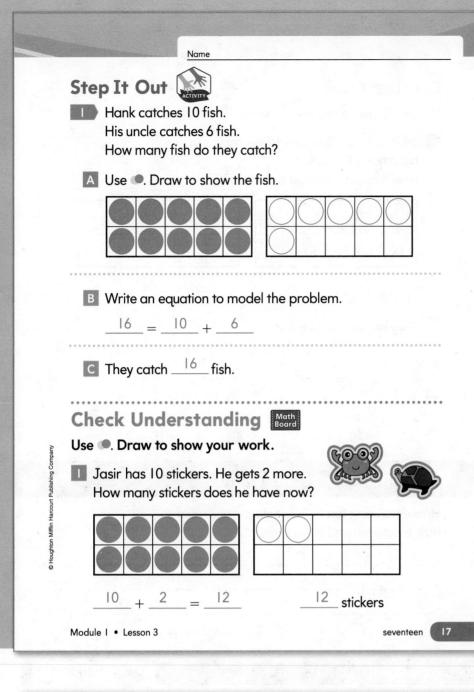

- -

B Write an equation to model the problem.

$$\underline{16} = \underline{10} + \underline{6}$$

- -

C They catch $\underline{16}$ fish.

• •

Check Understanding `Math Board`

Use ⬤. Draw to show your work.

1 Jasir has 10 stickers. He gets 2 more.
How many stickers does he have now?

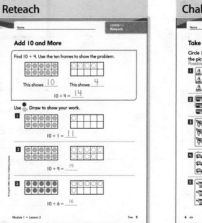

$$\underline{10} + \underline{2} = \underline{12}$$

$\underline{12}$ stickers

Module 1 • Lesson 3   seventeen **17**

Step It Out

Task 2 **MP** **Use Structure** The structure of the ten frames helps children quickly see the sum as a group of 10 and some more. Encourage children to count from 10 during this task instead of counting all 16 counters.

Sample Guided Discussion:

Q How many boxes in the first ten frame will you draw in to represent the fish that Hank catches? 10 boxes

Q How many boxes in the other ten frame will you draw in to represent the fish that his uncle catches? 6 boxes

Q How can you use the ten frames to find the sum? Possible answer: I will start with 10 since the first ten frame is full. Then I count 6 more.

---

data checkpoint

③ Check Understanding

Formative Assessment

Use formative assessment to determine if your children are successful with this lesson's learning objective.

Children who successfully complete the Check Understanding can continue to the On Your Own practice.

For children who missed the Check Understanding problem, work in a pulled small group with the Tabletop Flipchart Mini-Lesson.

ONLINE **Ed** **Assign the Digital Check Understanding to determine**
- success with the learning objective
- items to review
- grouping and differentiation resources

④ Differentiation Options

Differentiate instruction for all children using small-group mini-lessons and math center activities on page 15C.

Reteach | Challenge

Lesson 1.3   **17**

Assign the Digital On Your Own for
- built-in student supports
- Actionable Item Reports
- Standards Analysis Reports

On Your Own

- **Problem 2 · Use Tools** Children use counters and ten frames to represent the addition of 10 and a one-digit number.

- **Problems 3–6** Children practice adding 10 and a one-digit number.

(5) Wrap-Up

Summarize learning with your class. Consider using the Exit Ticket, Put It in Writing, or I Can scale.

Exit Ticket

Use counters in ten frames to represent the problem $10 + 8$. Write an addition equation and write the sum.

Check children's work.

$10 + 8 = 18$

Put It in Writing

Look at these equations. What patterns do you see?

$10 + 1 = 11$

$10 + 2 = 12$

$10 + 3 = 13$

I Can

The scale below can help you and your students understand their progress on a learning goal.

4	I can explain how to find the sum of 10 and some more.
3	I can find the sum of 10 and some more.
2	I can use ten frames to find the sum of 10 and some more by counting each filled box.
1	I can count forward from 10.

On Your Own

Use ⬤. Draw to show your work.

2 **Use Tools** Sam has 10 toy cars.
Bella has 8 toy cars.
How many toy cars do they have?

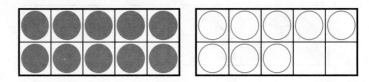

$10 + 8 = \underline{18}$

They have $\underline{18}$ toy cars.

Add.

3 $10 + 6 = \underline{16}$ 4 $10 + 9 = \underline{19}$

5 $\underline{10} = 10 + 0$ 6 $\underline{12} = 10 + 2$

🔲 I'm in a Learning Mindset!

How does using ten frames help me understand how to add ten and some more?

_____

_____

_____

Learning Mindset

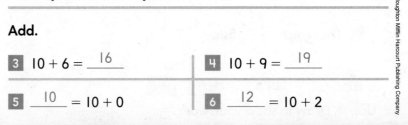

Try Again Collects and Tries Multiple Strategies

Remind children of the problems at the beginning of the lesson in which they represented and solved addition problems in different ways. Point out that they already have knowledge and strategies that can help them learn new things. *There are times you can use something you already know to help you learn something new. You know how to use ten frames to understand ten. Why do you think using ten frames is a good strategy for understanding how to add ten and some more?*

Assignment Guide

Reference the chart below for problems associated with tasks. In a 2-day lesson, reference the chart to assign daily homework.

Learn Together Tasks	On Your Own Problems
Task 1, p. 16	Problems 2–4
Task 2, p. 17	Problems 5 and 6

Name _____

LESSON 1.3
More Practice/ Homework

 **ONLINE**
Video Tutorials and
Interactive Examples

Add 10 and More

Draw ● to show your work.

1 (MP) **Use Tools** Ginger has 10 caps. *Check children's work.*
Then she gets 2 more caps.
How many caps does she have now?

$$\underline{10} + \underline{2} = \underline{12}$$

Ginger has __12__ caps now.

2 Draw ● to show 10. Draw ● to show 4.
Complete the equation to model the picture.

$$10 + \underline{4} = \underline{14}$$

Add.

3 $10 + 7 = \underline{17}$

4 $10 + 3 = \underline{13}$

5 $10 + 9 = \underline{19}$

6 $10 + 8 = \underline{18}$

7 $\underline{16} = 10 + 6$

8 $\underline{10} = 10 + 0$

ONLINE

Assign the Digital More Practice/
Homework for
• built-in student supports
• Actionable Item Reports
• Standards Analysis Reports

More Practice/Homework

Add 10 and More

Use More Practice/Homework pages to provide children
with additional practice applying the concepts and skills
presented in the lesson.

- **Problem 1 • Use Tools** Children show how ten frames
  can be used to add 10 and a one-digit number.

- **Problem 2** Children draw counters and complete an
  equation to show how to add 10 and a one-digit number.

- **Problems 3–8** Children add 10 and a one-digit number
  to solve computation problems.

Assignment Guide

Reference the chart below for problems associated with tasks. In a 2-day lesson,
reference the chart to assign daily homework.

Learn Together Tasks	More Practice/Homework Problems
Task 1, p. 16	Problems 1, 2, 3, 4, 5, 6, 9, 10, and 11
Task 2, p. 17	Problems 7, 8, and 11

Test Prep

The Test Prep items provided assess understanding of adding 10 and a one-digit number.

Additional Test Prep opportunities are available online and in *Getting Ready for High Stakes Assessments.*

Spiral Review

The spiral review problems will help determine if children have retained information taught in the past. Here, children will need to demonstrate the ability to count on to add. **(1.2)**

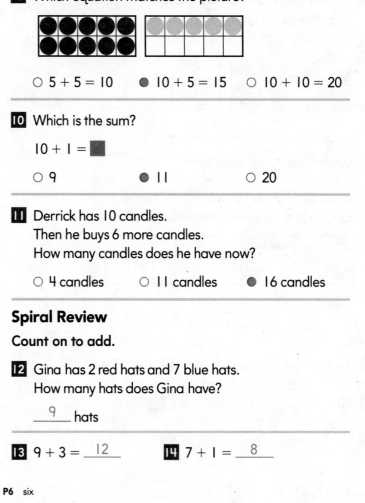

Test Prep

Fill in the bubble next to the correct answer.

9 Which equation matches the picture?

○ 5 + 5 = 10   ● 10 + 5 = 15   ○ 10 + 10 = 20

10 Which is the sum?

10 + 1 = ▉

○ 9   ● 11   ○ 20

11 Derrick has 10 candles.
Then he buys 6 more candles.
How many candles does he have now?

○ 4 candles   ○ 11 candles   ● 16 candles

Spiral Review

Count on to add.

12 Gina has 2 red hats and 7 blue hats.
How many hats does Gina have?

___9___ hats

13 9 + 3 = __12__   **14** 7 + 1 = __8__

1.4 Make a 10 to Add

LESSON FOCUS AND COHERENCE

■ Major ☐ Supporting ○ Additional

Mathematics Standards

■ Add and subtract within 20, demonstrating fluency for addition and subtraction within 10. Use strategies such as counting on; making ten (e.g., $8 + 6 = 8 + 2 + 4 = 10 + 4 = 14$); decomposing a number leading to a ten (e.g., $13 - 4 = 13 - 3 - 1 = 10 - 1 = 9$); using the relationship between addition and subtraction (e.g., knowing that $8 + 4 = 12$, one knows $12 - 8 = 4$); and creating equivalent but easier or known sums (e.g., adding $6 + 7$ by creating the known equivalent $6 + 6 + 1 = 12 + 1 = 13$).

Mathematical Practices and Processes (MP)

- Reason abstractly and quantitatively.
- Use appropriate tools strategically.
- Look for and make use of structure.

I Can Objective

I can use the make a ten strategy to help add.

Learning Objective

Use the *make a ten* strategy to solve addition facts.

Language Objectives

- Explain what *make a ten* means in context.
- Explain how to solve problems using the *make a ten* strategy.

Vocabulary

New: make a ten

Lesson Materials: two-color counters, Ten Frames (Teacher Resource Masters), pencils, crayons, MathBoard

Mathematical Progressions

Prior Learning	Current Development	Future Connections
Children: - broke apart numbers to 10 as the sum of two numbers. **(GrK, 13.4)** - used objects, drawings, and equations to represent ways to make 10. **(GrK, 7.4)**	**Children:** - apply the *make a ten* strategy to solve basic addition facts. - use concrete models such as counters and ten frames to represent addition.	**Children:** - will know all sums of two one-digit numbers by memory. **(Gr2, 1.2)** - will continue to explore the *make a ten* strategy to add within 20. **(Gr2, 1.5)** - will use mental strategies to fluently add within 20. **(Gr2, 1.2)**

PROFESSIONAL LEARNING

Using Mathematical Practices and Processes

Use appropriate tools strategically.

In this lesson, children will use several concrete and visual models to support their understanding of decomposing addends to make a ten. Using counters within a pair of ten frames is a common tool to make a ten because the first ten frame clearly shows the "ten" when it is full. As children progress through the lesson, have them reflect on the tools they have chosen to use and how the tools help them solve the problems. As children become more comfortable with the *make a ten* strategy, they may rely less on these tools and illustrate the strategy with equations instead of objects or pictures.

ACTIVATE PRIOR KNOWLEDGE • Make 10

Use these activities to quickly assess and activate prior knowledge as needed.

Math Routine

Building Numbers

Use ⬤. Show a way to make 10.
Then complete the equation.

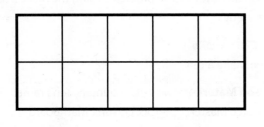

___ + ___ = 10

Allow children time to work out the problem above on their own. Provide children with counters and ten frames to show their thinking. They may also write or draw their responses on their MathBoards.

Invite children to share their answers with the class. Record their equations on the board. Ask for volunteers to share how they solved the problem. Have several children who used different strategies share their thinking with the class.

Then point to the ways to make 10 that you wrote on the board.
Ask: Did we miss any ways to make 10? How do you know?

Make Connections

Based on children's responses to the Math Routine, choose one of the following:

1 Project the Interactive Reteach, Grade K, Lesson 7.4.

2 Complete the Prerequisite Skills Activity:

Place 4 red counters within a ten frame. Guide children to find the number of counters that can be added to make 10. Write an equation together to represent the addition problem:
$4 + 6 = 10$.

Repeat by placing a different number of counters in the ten frame. Have children write an equation to represent addition with a sum of 10.

If children continue to struggle, use Tier 2 Skill 15.

SHARPEN SKILLS

If time permits, use this on-level activity to build fluency and practice basic skills.

Mental Math

Objective: Show ways to make 10.
Materials: Number Cards 0–10 (Teacher Resource Masters)

Use several sets of Number Cards. Give each child five cards. Explain that they will work together to find pairs of numbers that have a sum of 10. They should try to find as many pairs as possible. Children may use two of their own cards or one card of their own and one card from a classmate. Have children add the numbers without the aid of pencil and paper. The first child to use all of his or her cards wins. (If no child runs out of cards, the child with the fewest cards remaining wins.)

Small-Group Options

Use these teacher-guided activities with pulled small groups at the teacher table.

On Track

Materials: two-color counters, Ten Frames (Teacher Resource Masters)

Display the problem 7 + 5. Have children place 7 red counters inside the ten frame and 5 yellow counters outside the ten frame. Then have children move 3 of the yellow counters to complete the ten frame. Guide children to use the 10 counters in the ten frame and the 2 extra counters to write a new equation and find the sum.

Repeat the activity with 9 + 4. Invite children to explain the steps to make a ten.

Almost There   (Rtl)

Materials: two-color counters, Ten Frames (Teacher Resource Masters)

Use this Tabletop Flipchart Mini-Lesson to guide children as they use counters and a ten frame to demonstrate how to efficiently add two one-digit numbers by making a ten and some ones.

Tabletop Flipchart:
Lesson 1.4

Mini-Lesson

Ready for More

Materials: Ten Frames (Teacher Resource Masters), connecting cubes

Provide children with a one-digit addition problem with a sum greater than 10 (such as 8 + 7). Invite children to show how to solve the problem using connecting cubes, a ten frame, and the *make a ten* strategy. After they make a ten, have children use the cubes inside the ten frame to form a cube train with 10 cubes. Have them name the number represented by the cube train and the extra cubes.

Math Center Options

Use these student self-directed activities at centers or stations.   **Key: ● Print Resources ● Online Resources**

On Track

- ●● More Practice/Homework 1.4
- ● My Learning Summary
- ● Interactive Glossary: **make a ten**

Almost There

- ● Reteach 1.4
- ● Interactive Reteach 1.4
- ●● Rtl Tier 2 Skill 15: Make Groups of 10
- ● Poggles MX: Addition and Subtraction, Level 14, Partners of 10

Ready for More

- ● Challenge 1.4
- ● Interactive Challenge 1.4

ONLINE ☺Ed   View data-driven grouping recommendations and assign differentiation resources.

During the *Spark Your Learning,* listen and watch for strategies students use. See samples of student work on this page.

Ways to Make 10 — Strategy 1

$$5 + 5 = 10$$

$$3 + 7 = 10$$

$$7 + 3 = 10$$

$$6 + 4 = 10$$

$$2 + 8 = 10$$

If children . . . show five different ways to make 10, they are demonstrating exemplary understanding of making 10.

Have these children . . . share and explain how they know each way makes 10. **Ask:**

Q What do you notice about your different ways to make 10?

Duplicate Ways to Make 10 — Strategy 2

$$4 + 6 = 10$$

$$3 + 7 = 10$$

$$1 + 9 = 10$$

$$4 + 6 = 10$$

$$1 + 9 = 10$$

If children . . . show ways to make 10 but repeat some equations, encourage them to consider how to modify the equations to avoid duplicates.

Activate prior knowledge . . . by prompting children to consider how patterns can help them write the ways to make 10. **Ask:**

Q How can you use a pattern to make different ways to make 10?

COMMON ERROR: Sums Greater Than 10

$$2 + 9 = 10$$

$$8 + 2 = 10$$

$$3 + 8 = 10$$

$$7 + 4 = 10$$

$$5 + 7 = 10$$

If children . . . include pairs of addends that have a sum greater than 10, they may not understand that "making ten" involves finding two addends that add up to an exact sum of 10.

Then intervene . . . by reminding children to think about 10 as the total, or sum, of the problem. **Ask:**

Q What does it mean if 10 is the sum?

Q What numbers can you show that add up to a total of 10?

Q Should any of your ways make more than 10?

Name _____

Make a 10 to Add

(I Can) use the make a ten strategy to help add.

Spark Your Learning

How can you make 10 in different ways?

Check children's work.

____ + ____ = 10

____ + ____ = 10

____ + ____ = 10

____ + ____ = 10

____ + ____ = 10

Have children work in small groups to find different ways to make 10.
Have them record their work. Discuss how there are many different
combinations of numbers that can be used to make 10.

Module 1 • Lesson 4

nineteen   19

---

① Spark Your Learning

▶ MOTIVATE

Introduce the problem by reading it aloud. **Ask:** What do
you know about the number 10?

▶ PERSEVERE

If children need support, guide them by asking:

Q **Assessing** What will both of your numbers add to? 10

Q **Assessing** When you write one number, what can you
think to help find the second number? Possible answer:
How many more do I need to make 10?

Q **Assessing** What two numbers can you add to make
10? Possible answer: 4 and 6

Q **Advancing • Use Tools** Which tool could you use to
solve the problem? Why is the tool you chose the one
that works for you? Children's choices of strategies or
tools will vary.

Q **Advancing • Use Tools** How can a ten frame help you
show your ways to make 10? Possible answer: I can use
red counters to show one number and yellow counters
to show the other number. If the numbers make 10,
then the counters fill the ten frame.

Turn and Talk Can you make a pattern as
you write your ways to make 10? Explain.
Possible answer: Yes. The first numbers in the equations
can be 1, 2, 3, 4, 5. The second numbers in the equations
can be 9, 8, 7, 6, 5.

▶ BUILD SHARED UNDERSTANDING

Select children who have used various strategies and tools
to share with the class how they solved the problem. Have
children discuss why they chose a specific strategy or tool.

② Learn Together

Build Understanding

Task 1 **(MP)** **Use Tools** The ten frame is a tool that children may choose to use to make a ten because it always shows a group of 10 when it is full.

CONNECT TO VOCABULARY

Have children use the **Interactive Glossary** during this conversation to record their understanding.

(EL) **CONNECT MATH IDEAS, REASONING, AND LANGUAGE** Compare and Connect

Have children describe the meaning of **make a ten** in their own words. Have partners share their work and discuss how their descriptions compare and contrast.

Sample Guided Discussion:

Q How can you show 7 and 5 as separate groups?
Possible answer: use red and yellow counters

Q Start with 7 counters in the ten frame. How many more counters can be added to make 10? 3 How many counters are left to add? 2

Turn and Talk Allow children to refer to their work in Parts A and B as they respond. Possible answer: I added 3 to 7 to make 10. I want to add 5 in all, so I still need to add 2 more.

Build Understanding

Kayla has 7 red flowers.
She has 5 yellow flowers.
How many flowers does she have?

A How can you make a ten to show the problem?

Possible answer shown.

B How can you complete the equations to solve the problem?

$10 + \underline{2} = \underline{12}$

So, $7 + 5 = \underline{12}$.

C Kayla has $\underline{12}$ flowers.

Connect to Vocabulary

make a ten

$8 + 4 = 12$

Turn and Talk What did you add to 7 to make 10? What did you still need to add? Explain.
See possible answer at the left.

© Houghton Mifflin Harcourt Publishing Company

LEVELED QUESTIONS

Depth of Knowledge (DOK)	Leveled Questions	What Does This Tell You?
Level 1 **Recall**	How many counters do you need to fill a ten frame? 10	Children's answers to this question will demonstrate whether they understand that a full ten frame represents a quantity of 10.
Level 2 **Basic Application of Skills & Concepts**	When you add 7 and 5, how many of the 5 counters are left over when you use some of them to make 10? 2	Children's answers to this question will demonstrate whether they can decompose an addend into the amount needed to make a ten and the remaining amount that will be added to the ten.
Level 3 **Strategic Thinking & Complex Reasoning**	Why is the *make a ten* strategy faster than counting each counter in your concrete model? Possible answer: If I make a ten, I count from 10. If I count each counter, I have to start from 1, and that takes more time.	Children's answers to this question will demonstrate whether they can explain why the *make a ten* strategy can be a more efficient way to add than counting.

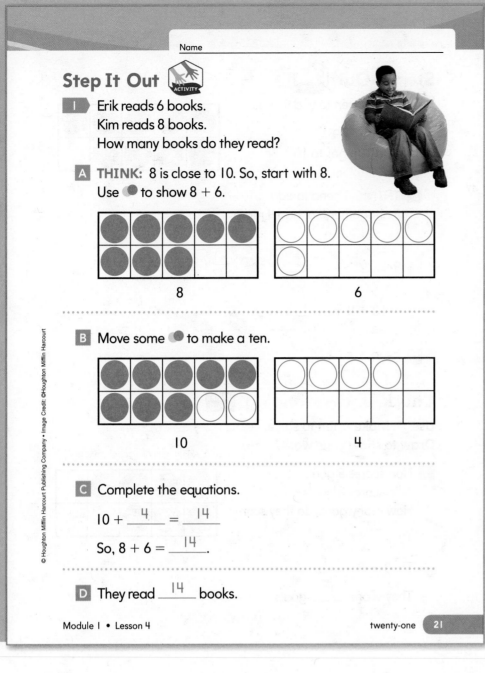

Step It Out

1 Erik reads 6 books.
Kim reads 8 books.
How many books do they read?

A THINK: 8 is close to 10. So, start with 8.
Use ⚫ to show 8 + 6.

8   6

B Move some ⚫ to make a ten.

10   4

C Complete the equations.

10 + __4__ = __14__

So, 8 + 6 = __14__.

D They read __14__ books.

Step It Out

Task 2 **MP** **Use Structure** In Part A, children represent the addends in separate ten frames. When they move some of the counters to make a ten in Part B, the structure of the ten frames helps them quickly see the sum as a group of ten with 4 more.

Sample Guided Discussion:

Q Why does it make sense to start with 8 counters in Part A instead of 6 counters? Possible answer: Since I'm making a ten, I want to show the number closest to 10 first. It's faster to make a ten that way.

Q How can you show the number 8 and the number 6 differently in your concrete model? Possible answer: I can use red and yellow counters.

Q What part of 8 + 6 matches the 8 counters you placed in the ten frame? the first number I add, 8

Q How many counters do you need to move from the second ten frame to the first ten frame to make a ten? 2

Q How many of the 6 counters in the second ten frame are remaining after you make a ten? 4

Q What equation can you use to represent the counters in Part B? Possible answer: 10 + 4 = 14

Step It Out

Task 3 **MP** **Reason** Make sure children connect the quantitative reasoning presented in Parts A and B with the more abstract reasoning presented in Parts C and D.

Sample Guided Discussion:

Q Why does it make sense to start with 9 instead of 5?
Possible answer: 9 is closer to 10, so it's faster to make a ten if I start with 9.

Q How many more counters do you need to add to 9 to make a ten? 1

Q How does the ten frame help you see the ten?
Possible answer: I can see that there is 1 box that needs to be filled to complete the frame, and I know that each frame is equal to 10 when it is full.

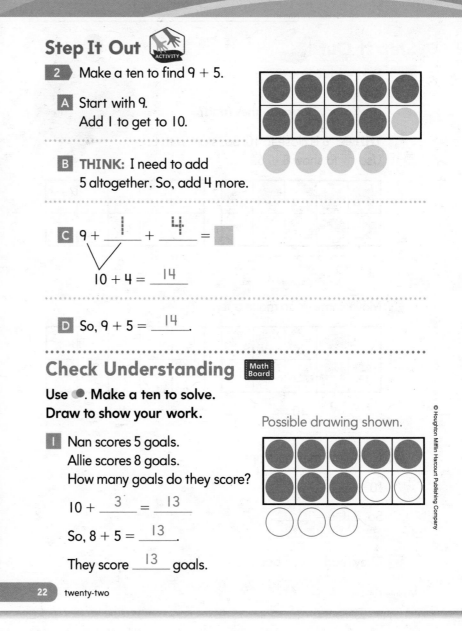

Step It Out

2 Make a ten to find $9 + 5$.

A Start with 9.
Add 1 to get to 10.

B THINK: I need to add 5 altogether. So, add 4 more.

C $9 + \underline{} + \underline{} = \blacksquare$

$10 + 4 = \underline{14}$

D So, $9 + 5 = \underline{14}$.

Check Understanding Math Board

Use ●. Make a ten to solve.
Draw to show your work.

Possible drawing shown.

1 Nan scores 5 goals.
Allie scores 8 goals.
How many goals do they score?

$10 + \underline{3} = \underline{13}$

So, $8 + 5 = \underline{13}$.

They score $\underline{13}$ goals.

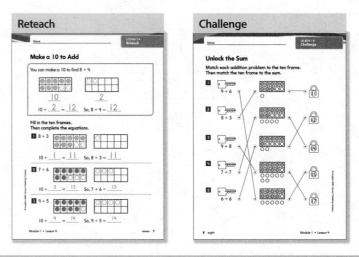

22   twenty-two

(3) Check Understanding

Formative Assessment

Use formative assessment to determine if your children are successful with this lesson's learning objective.

Children who successfully complete the Check Understanding can continue to the On Your Own practice.

For children who missed the Check Understanding problem, work in a pulled small group with the Tabletop Flipchart Mini-Lesson.

ONLINE **Ed**   **Assign the Digital Check Understanding to determine**
- success with the learning objective
- items to review
- grouping and differentiation resources

(4) Differentiation Options

Differentiate instruction for all children using small-group mini-lessons and math center activities on page 19C.

Reteach

Challenge

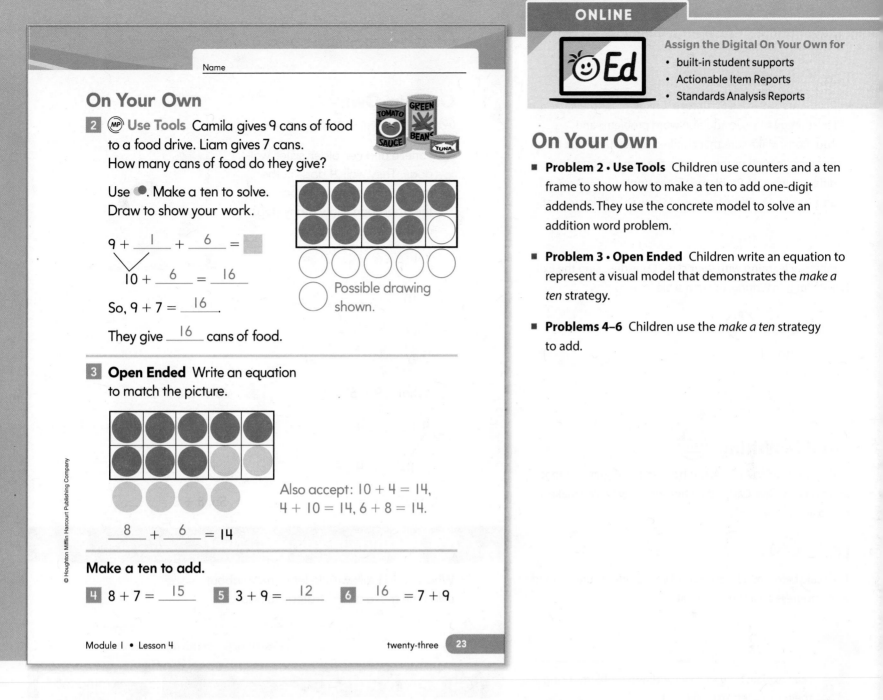

On Your Own

2 (MP) **Use Tools** Camila gives 9 cans of food to a food drive. Liam gives 7 cans. How many cans of food do they give?

Use ⬤. Make a ten to solve. Draw to show your work.

$9 + \underline{1} + \underline{6} = $ ▢

$10 + \underline{6} = \underline{16}$

So, $9 + 7 = \underline{16}$.

They give $\underline{16}$ cans of food.

Possible drawing shown.

3 **Open Ended** Write an equation to match the picture.

Also accept: $10 + 4 = 14$, $4 + 10 = 14$, $6 + 8 = 14$.

$\underline{8} + \underline{6} = 14$

Make a ten to add.

4 $8 + 7 = \underline{15}$ **5** $3 + 9 = \underline{12}$ **6** $\underline{16} = 7 + 9$

Assign the Digital On Your Own for
- built-in student supports
- Actionable Item Reports
- Standards Analysis Reports

On Your Own

- **Problem 2 • Use Tools** Children use counters and a ten frame to show how to make a ten to add one-digit addends. They use the concrete model to solve an addition word problem.

- **Problem 3 • Open Ended** Children write an equation to represent a visual model that demonstrates the *make a ten* strategy.

- **Problems 4–6** Children use the *make a ten* strategy to add.

Assignment Guide

Reference the chart below for problems associated with tasks. In a 2-day lesson, reference the chart to assign daily homework.

Learn Together Tasks	On Your Own Problems
Tasks 1 and 2, pp. 20–21	Problems 3–6
Task 3, p. 22	Problems 2, 4, 5, 6, 7, 8, and 9

On Your Own

■ **Problems 7–9 · Use Structure** Children use the *make a ten* strategy to solve addition word problems and equations. Make sure that children understand that the numbers in each problem show the same amount in different ways. In Problem 7, for example, 7 + 4, 7 + 3 + 1, and 10 + 1 are different ways to show the same amount.

⑤ Wrap-Up

Summarize learning with your class. Consider using the Exit Ticket, Put It in Writing, or I Can scale.

Exit Ticket

Make a ten to solve.

$6 + 7 =$ ▪

13; Check children's work.

Put It in Writing ✎

Carlos wants to add 8 + 4, but he does not remember that addition fact. Give Carlos directions for how he can make a ten to add 8 + 4.

I Can

The scale below can help you and your students understand their progress on a learning goal.

4	I can explain how to solve addition problems using the make a ten strategy.
3	I can use the make a ten strategy to help add.
2	I can use a ten frame to help add one-digit numbers.
1	I can use counters and a ten frame to make 10.

On Your Own

(MP) Use Structure **Make a ten to solve.**

7 Janelle and her older sister walk dogs. They walk 4 dogs in the morning. They walk 7 dogs in the afternoon. How many dogs do they walk?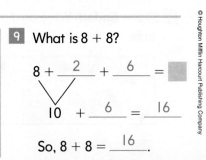

$$7 + \underline{3} + \underline{1} = \blacksquare$$

$$10 + 1 = \underline{11}$$

So, $7 + 4 = \underline{11}$.

They walk $\underline{11}$ dogs.

8 What is 9 + 5?	**9** What is 8 + 8?
$9 + \underline{1} + \underline{4} = \blacksquare$	$8 + \underline{2} + \underline{6} = \blacksquare$
$10 + 4 = \underline{14}$	$10 + \underline{6} = \underline{16}$
So, $9 + 5 = \underline{14}$.	So, $8 + 8 = \underline{16}$.

⬡ I'm in a Learning Mindset!

Who should I talk with to learn more about using the make a ten strategy to add?

_____

Learning Mindset

mindset works

Try Again Checks for Understanding

This lesson required children to think flexibly and extend their understanding in new ways. The conceptual nature of this skill can be frustrating for some children, particularly for those who have difficulty thinking abstractly or for those who can already add the quantities without the use of this strategy. Facilitate a discussion that acknowledges the challenges with which children were presented and reflect on the progress they made throughout the lesson. *It is important to know what you found challenging about using a strategy so that you can find the right type of help. Sometimes finding the right person to talk to is the type of help you need. Some children in this class may have already found out that using this strategy is a little bit like using ten frames to add 10 and some more. Find a partner and talk about it.*

Name _____

LESSON 1.4
More Practice/
Homework

ONLINE
Video Tutorials and
Interactive Examples

Make a Ten to Add

1 **Open Ended** Write an equation
to match the picture.

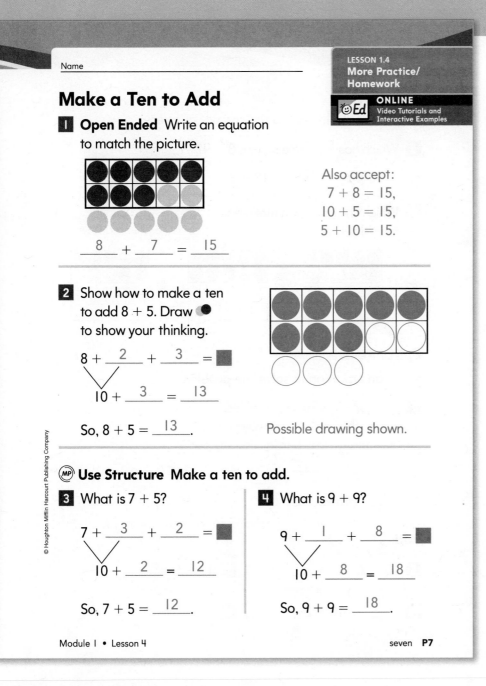

Also accept:
$7 + 8 = 15$,
$10 + 5 = 15$,
$5 + 10 = 15$.

___8___ + ___7___ = ___15___

2 Show how to make a ten
to add $8 + 5$. Draw ●
to show your thinking.

$8 + \underset{\diagdown\diagup}{2} + 3 = \blacksquare$

$10 + ___3___ = ___13___$

So, $8 + 5 = ___13___$.

Possible drawing shown.

MP **Use Structure** Make a ten to add.

3 What is $7 + 5$?

$7 + \underset{\diagdown\diagup}{3} + 2 = \blacksquare$

$10 + ___2___ = ___12___$

So, $7 + 5 = ___12___$.

4 What is $9 + 9$?

$9 + \underset{\diagdown\diagup}{1} + 8 = \blacksquare$

$10 + ___8___ = ___18___$

So, $9 + 9 = ___18___$.

ONLINE

Assign the Digital More Practice/
Homework for
• built-in student supports
• Actionable Item Reports
• Standards Analysis Reports

More Practice/Homework

Make a Ten to Add

Use More Practice/Homework pages to provide children
with additional practice applying the concepts and skills
presented in the lesson.

- **Problem 1 • Open Ended** Children write an equation to
  represent a visual model that demonstrates the *make a
  ten* strategy.

- **Problem 2** Children draw and complete equations to
  demonstrate the *make a ten* strategy.

- **Problems 3 and 4 • Use Structure** Children use the
  make a ten strategy to solve addition equations.

Assignment Guide

Reference the chart below for problems associated with tasks. In a 2-day lesson,
reference the chart to assign daily homework.

Learn Together Tasks	More Practice/Homework Problems
Tasks 1 and 2, pp. 20–21	Problems 1, 5, and 6
Task 3, p. 22	Problems 2–6

Test Prep

The Test Prep items provided assess understanding of making a ten to add.

Additional Test Prep opportunities are available online and in *Getting Ready for High Stakes Assessments.*

Spiral Review

The spiral review problems will help determine if children have retained information taught in the past. Here, children will need to demonstrate the ability to add 10 and a one-digit number. **(1.3)**

© Houghton Mifflin Harcourt Publishing Company

Test Prep

Fill in the bubble next to the correct answer.

5 Which has the same sum as 8 + 4?

   ○ 10 + 6   ○ 10 + 3   ● 10 + 2

6 Which shows how to make a ten to add 5 + 9?

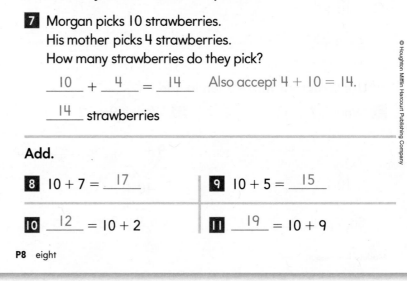

Spiral Review

Write an equation to solve the problem.

7 Morgan picks 10 strawberries.
His mother picks 4 strawberries.
How many strawberries do they pick?

   __10__ + __4__ = __14__   Also accept 4 + 10 = 14.

   __14__ strawberries

Add.

8 10 + 7 = __17__   **9** 10 + 5 = __15__

10 __12__ = 10 + 2   **11** __19__ = 10 + 9

1.5 Add Doubles

LESSON FOCUS AND COHERENCE

■ Major ☐ Supporting ○ Additional

Mathematics Standards

■ Add and subtract within 20, demonstrating fluency for addition and subtraction within 10. Use strategies such as counting on; making ten (e.g., $8 + 6 = 8 + 2 + 4 = 10 + 4 = 14$); decomposing a number leading to a ten (e.g., $13 - 4 = 13 - 3 - 1 = 10 - 1 = 9$); using the relationship between addition and subtraction (e.g., knowing that $8 + 4 = 12$, one knows $12 - 8 = 4$); and creating equivalent but easier or known sums (e.g., adding $6 + 7$ by creating the known equivalent $6 + 6 + 1 = 12 + 1 = 13$).

Mathematical Practices and Processes (MP)

- Look for and make use of structure.
- Look for and express regularity in repeated reasoning.

I Can Objective

I can identify, represent, and solve doubles facts.

Learning Objective

Represent and solve doubles facts.

Language Objectives

- Explain what a doubles fact is.
- Explain how to solve problems using doubles facts.

Vocabulary

New: doubles

Lesson Materials: connecting cubes, two-color counters, crayons, pencils, MathBoard

Mathematical Progressions

Prior Learning	Current Development	Future Connections
Children: - solved addition word problems within 10. **(GrK, 11.3)** - represented addition within 10 using objects, drawings, and equations. **(GrK, 11.3, 11.5, 12.1, and 12.3)**	**Children:** - use doubles facts to solve addition problems. - use objects, drawings, and equations to represent doubles facts.	**Children:** - will use known doubles facts to find the sums of other facts. **(Gr2, 1.1)** - will use mental strategies to fluently add within 20. **(Gr2, 1.2)** - will know all sums of two one-digit numbers by memory. **(Gr2, 1.2)**

PROFESSIONAL LEARNING

Using Mathematical Practices and Processes

Look for and make use of structure.

In this lesson, children will analyze the structure of equations and recognize the significance of addition facts in which a number is added to itself. They will learn to identify and use doubles facts to help solve addition problems. They will start by making doubles of their own visually and then will solve doubles facts with an unknown sum.

In the next lesson, children extend this work as they use the structure of doubles facts to find the sums of other addition facts (by adding 1 to the sum of a doubles fact).

ACTIVATE PRIOR KNOWLEDGE • Represent Addition

Use these activities to quickly assess and activate prior knowledge as needed.

Math Routine

Building Numbers

How can you show two groups that make a total of 8?

Display the problem above and have children solve it on their own. Children may write or draw their responses on their MathBoards or use any available tools, such as their fingers, connecting cubes, ten frames, counters, or a rekenrek. Encourage a variety of responses, such as equations, drawings, and concrete models.

Have children share their representations with the class and ask them to compare their work. Have them tell how their representation differed from a classmate's. For example, one child might show 5 red counters and 3 yellow counters in a ten frame while another child writes $2 + 6 = 8$.

Repeat for other numbers up to 10 as time allows.

Make Connections

Based on children's responses to the Math Routine, choose one of the following:

1 Project the Interactive Reteach, Grade K, Lesson 5.3.

2 Complete the Prerequisite Skills Activity:

Write $4 + 1$ on the board. Tell children there are many ways they can represent this, such as with a picture. Draw 4 circles on the board. Draw 1 circle on the board. Guide children to count each of the 5 circles to find the total.

Have children work in pairs to represent the same problem with counters or connecting cubes. If time permits, have them show a different addition problem, using a different kind of representation.

If children continue to struggle, use Tier 3 Skill 5.

SHARPEN SKILLS

If time permits, use this on-level activity to build fluency and practice basic skills.

Mental Math

Objective: Add within 5 using mental math.

Have children add $5 + 0 = \underline{}5\underline{}$, $4 + 1 = 5$, and $3 + 2 = \underline{}5\underline{}$.

Ask: What is the sum of $2 + 3$? How do you know? 5; Possible answers: I have that fact memorized; $2 + 3$ adds the same two numbers as $3 + 2$, so the sum has to be the same.

Small-Group Options

Use these teacher-guided activities with pulled small groups at the teacher table.

On Track

Materials: connecting cubes

Have children sit in a circle. One child passes a number of connecting cubes to the left (1 to 9 cubes). The second child makes an identical group of cubes and then passes both groups of cubes to the left. The third child uses the two identical groups to write and solve a doubles fact.

Repeat the activity two more times, so that each child takes a turn writing and solving a doubles fact.

Almost There (RtI)

Materials: connecting cubes

Use this Tabletop Flipchart Mini-Lesson to guide children as they represent doubles facts using addition equations and equal groups of connecting cubes.

Tabletop Flipchart:
Lesson 1.5

Mini-Lesson

Ready for More

Challenge children to find classroom objects that can be represented by doubles facts. Point out that the objects should show two equal groups. Examples may include dominoes with an equal number of dots on each side, fingers on gloves (5 fingers on each glove), or shoelace holes on a shoe (4 shoelace holes on each side of a shoe).

Then have children name the doubles fact that matches each object.

Math Center Options

Use these student self-directed activities at centers or stations.   **Key:** ● Print Resources ● Online Resources

On Track

- ●● More Practice/Homework 1.5
- ● Fluency Builder: Addition Level 1
- ● Interactive Glossary: **doubles**

Almost There

- ● Reteach 1.5
- ● Interactive Reteach 1.5
- ●● RtI Tier 3 Skill 5: Model Addition

Ready for More

- ● Challenge 1.5
- ● Interactive Challenge 1.5

ONLINE ☺ **Ed**   View data-driven grouping recommendations and assign differentiation resources.

During the *Spark Your Learning,* listen and watch for strategies students use. See samples of student work on this page.

Doubles Facts   Strategy 1

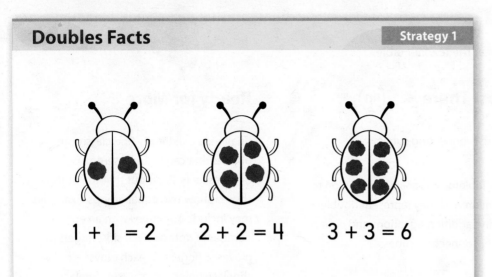

1 + 1 = 2   2 + 2 = 4   3 + 3 = 6

If children . . . correctly draw matching pairs of spots and write facts with matching addends, they are demonstrating exemplary understanding of doubles facts.

Have these children . . . share and explain how they solved the problem. **Ask:**

Q How did you know how many spots to draw?

Q What do you notice about the numbers you add in each of your equations?

Duplicate Doubles Facts   Strategy 2

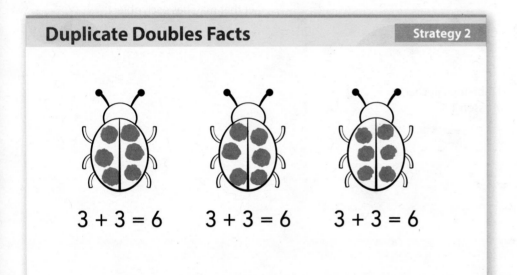

3 + 3 = 6   3 + 3 = 6   3 + 3 = 6

If children . . . make all ladybugs into the same doubles fact, they may need some assistance coming up with a variety of solutions to the problem.

Activate prior knowledge . . . by encouraging them to think of other doubles facts. **Ask:**

Q How can you make the spots on the ladybugs look different from each other?

Q If there is only 1 spot on the left side, how many spots should be on the right side?

Q What is the rule for how many spots to draw?

COMMON ERROR: Unequal Groups

1 + 2 = 3   2 + 2 = 4   2 + 3 = 5

If children . . . draw too many or too few spots on one side of the ladybug, they may have difficulty interpreting the problem.

Then intervene . . . by reminding children to draw the same number of spots on both sides of each ladybug. **Ask:**

Q How many spots did you draw on the left side?

Q How many spots should be on the right side?

Name _____

Add Doubles

(I Can) identify, represent, and solve doubles facts.

Spark Your Learning

Ladybugs have the same number
of spots on each side of their bodies.
Draw to show all the spots on each ladybug.

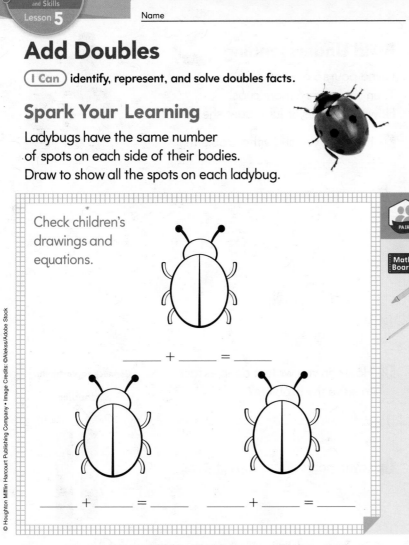

Check children's
drawings and
equations.

_____ + _____ = _____

_____ + _____ = _____   _____ + _____ = _____

Have children draw to show a different total number of spots on each ladybug
and write the equation to model the addition. Remind children that there
should be the same number of spots on each side of each ladybug.

Module 1 • Lesson 5   twenty-five **25**

---

① Spark Your Learning

▶ MOTIVATE

Introduce the problem by reading it aloud. **Ask:** What do
you know about ladybugs? Have children talk about
ladybugs they have seen or heard about.

EL **SUPPORT SENSE-MAKING Three Reads**
Read the problem three times for children. Ask
children a different question shown in the Three Reads box
below for a different focus each time.

▶ PERSEVERE

If children need support, guide them by asking:

Q **Assessing** What does *same number on each side*
mean? Possible answer: The number of spots on each
side should be equal.

Q **Assessing** How many spots should you draw on the
first side of the blank ladybug? Possible answer: any
number I want as long as I count how many I drew

Q **Assessing** How many spots should you draw on the
second side of the blank ladybug? the same number I
drew on the first side

Q **Assessing** What numbers will you write in the
equation? the number of spots on each side and the
total number of spots

Q **Advancing • Use Tools** Which tool could you use to
solve the problem? Why is the tool you chose the one
that works for you? Children's choices of strategies and
tools will vary.

Q **Advancing** What is the same about the equations
you wrote? Possible answer: Each equation has two
addends that are the same.

 Turn and Talk Can a ladybug have a total of
9 spots? Why or why not? no; Possible answer:
because 4 spots on both sides makes 8 and 5 spots on
both sides makes 10

▶ BUILD SHARED UNDERSTANDING

Select children who have used various strategies and tools
to share with the class how they solved the problem. Have
children discuss why they chose a specific strategy or tool.

EL ## SUPPORT SENSE-MAKING • Three Reads

Read the problem stem three times and prompt the children with a different
question each time.

1 What is the problem about?
the number of spots on ladybugs

2 What do each of the numbers describe?
The first two numbers in each equation describe how many spots are on each
side of the ladybug. The last number in each equation describes the total
number of spots on the ladybug.

3 What math questions could you ask about the problem?
Possible questions: How many spots are on one side of the ladybug? How many
spots are on the other side? How do you find the sum?

© Houghton Mifflin Harcourt Publishing Company • Image Credits: ©Aleksx/Adobe Stock

(2) Learn Together

Build Understanding

Task 1 **(MP)** **Use Structure** Present children with several doubles facts so they can see that the structure of all doubles facts are similar, with two identical addends.

CONNECT TO VOCABULARY

Have children use the **Interactive Glossary** during this conversation to record their understanding.

(EL) **CONNECT MATH IDEAS, REASONING, AND LANGUAGE** **Compare and Connect**

Have children describe the meaning of **doubles** in their own words. Have partners share their work and discuss how their descriptions compare and contrast.

Sample Guided Discussion:

Q **How can you draw to represent this problem?** Possible answer: draw two groups with 6 circles in each group

Q **What makes this addition fact a doubles fact?** Possible answer: Both numbers I add are the same (6).

Turn and Talk If children are not sure how to answer the question, encourage them to look at the two numbers they added in the equation they wrote. Possible answer: The numbers are the same.

Build Understanding

Layna pours 6 cups of juice.
Then she pours 6 more cups.
How many cups of juice does she pour?

A How can you show the problem?

Possible answer shown.

B How can you write a doubles fact to solve the problem?

$$\underline{6} + \underline{6} = \underline{12}$$

C Layna pours ___12___ cups of juice.

Connect to Vocabulary

doubles
$$5 + 5 = 10$$

Turn and Talk What do you notice about the numbers you are adding? See possible answer at the left.

LEVELED QUESTIONS

Depth of Knowledge (DOK)	Leveled Questions	What Does This Tell You?
Level 1 **Recall**	Is $3 + 6$ a doubles fact? Explain. no; Possible answer: 3 and 6 are different numbers. A doubles fact adds two numbers that are the same.	Children's answers to this question will demonstrate whether they understand what doubles are.
Level 2 **Basic Application of Skills & Concepts**	How could you write a doubles fact for the problem if there were 4 cups and 4 more? $4 + 4 = 8$ or $8 = 4 + 4$	Children's answers to this question will demonstrate whether they can write an equation for doubles.
Level 3 **Strategic Thinking & Complex Reasoning**	Use doubles to tell a different word problem about Layna pouring cups of juice. What doubles fact can you write to solve? Possible answer: Layna pours 8 cups. Then she pours 8 more. How many does she pour? $8 + 8 = 16$	Children's answers to this question will demonstrate whether they understand doubles and can make new doubles problems on their own.

Step It Out

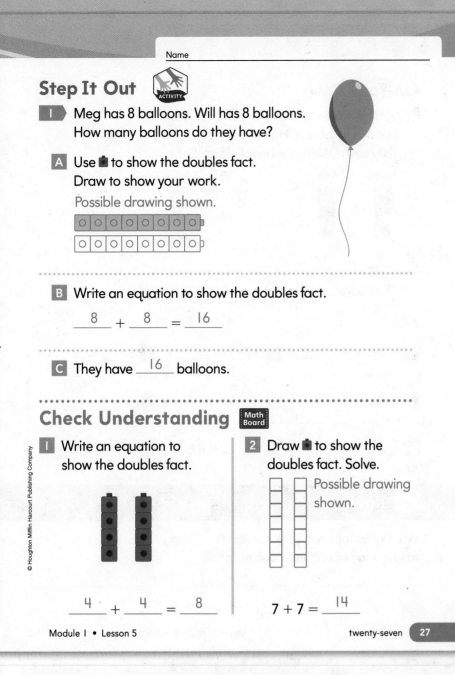

1 Meg has 8 balloons. Will has 8 balloons. How many balloons do they have?

A Use ▮ to show the doubles fact. Draw to show your work.

Possible drawing shown.

B Write an equation to show the doubles fact.

$$\underline{\quad 8 \quad} + \underline{\quad 8 \quad} = \underline{\quad 16 \quad}$$

C They have $\underline{\quad 16 \quad}$ balloons.

Check Understanding Math Board

1 Write an equation to show the doubles fact.

$$\underline{\quad 4 \quad} + \underline{\quad 4 \quad} = \underline{\quad 8 \quad}$$

2 Draw ▮ to show the doubles fact. Solve.

Possible drawing shown.

$$7 + 7 = \underline{\quad 14 \quad}$$

Module 1 • Lesson 5   twenty-seven **27**

© Houghton Mifflin Harcourt Publishing Company

Step It Out

Task 2 (MP) **Use Repeated Reasoning** As children become more comfortable with doubles facts, they should generalize that the two numbers added together in any doubles fact are always the same.

Sample Guided Discussion:

Q **What does each connecting cube represent?**
1 balloon

Q **Why did you show the connecting cubes as two equal groups?** Possible answer: because Megan and Will have equal groups of balloons

Q **How do you model the problem with addition?**
Possible answer: I write an addition equation to show that Meg's ballons plus Will's balloons is equal to the total number of balloons they have.

Q **How do you know the equation you wrote is a doubles fact?** Possible answer: The two numbers that I add are the same, 8.

data
checkpoint

---

③ Check Understanding

Formative Assessment

Use formative assessment to determine if your children are successful with this lesson's learning objective.

Children who successfully complete the Check Understanding can continue to the On Your Own practice.

For children who miss 1 problem or more, work in a pulled small group with the Tabletop Flipchart Mini-Lesson.

ONLINE **Ed**

Assign the Digital Check Understanding to determine
- success with the learning objective
- items to review
- grouping and differentiation resources

④ Differentiation Options

Differentiate instruction for all children using small-group mini-lessons and math center activities on page 25C.

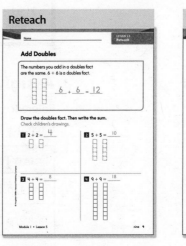

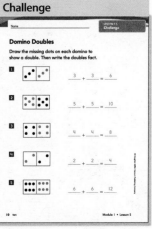

Assign the Digital On Your Own for
- built-in student supports
- Actionable Item Reports
- Standards Analysis Reports

On Your Own

- **Problem 3 · Use Structure** Children write a doubles fact to match a visual model and solve a word problem.

- **Problems 4–12** Children find the sums of doubles facts.

⑤ Wrap-Up

Summarize learning with your class. Consider using the Exit Ticket, Put It in Writing, or I Can scale.

Exit Ticket 🔘

What is the sum of the doubles fact $9 + 9$? 18

Put It in Writing 📝

How can you recognize doubles facts?

I Can 🔘

The scale below can help you and your students understand their progress on a learning goal.

4	I can explain how doubles facts can be used to solve problems.
3	I can identify, represent, and solve doubles facts.
2	I can represent doubles facts using objects or pictures.
1	I can tell when an addition fact is a doubles fact.

On Your Own

3 (MP) **Use Structure** Maya has 3 ribbons. Lee has 3 ribbons. How many ribbons do they have? Write the doubles fact. Solve.

Maya   Lee

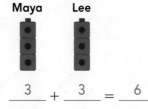

$$\underline{\quad 3 \quad} + \underline{\quad 3 \quad} = \underline{\quad 6 \quad}$$

They have ___6___ ribbons.

Add.

4 $1 + 1 = \underline{\ 2\ }$	**5** $7 + 7 = \underline{\ 14\ }$	**6** $5 + 5 = \underline{\ 10\ }$
7 $2 + 2 = \underline{\ 4\ }$	**8** $9 + 9 = \underline{\ 18\ }$	**9** $6 + 6 = \underline{\ 12\ }$
10 $\underline{\ 8\ } = 4 + 4$	**11** $\underline{\ 16\ } = 8 + 8$	**12** $\underline{\ 6\ } = 3 + 3$

© Houghton Mifflin Harcourt Publishing Company

⚛ I'm in a Learning Mindset!

What questions can I ask my teacher to help me understand doubles facts?

_____

_____

Learning Mindset

mindset works

Try Again Collects and Tries Multiple Strategies

Explain to children that asking questions can be a strategy for learning. *You can ask questions to help you understand doubles facts. Do not ask a question just to have someone tell you the answer. When you ask a question, the answer should help you understand enough to do the work on your own. That way, you will be able to use what you learned on any problem of the same type instead of only knowing the answer to a single problem.*

Assignment Guide

Reference the chart below for problems associated with tasks. In a 2-day lesson, reference the chart to assign daily homework.

Learn Together Tasks	On Your Own Problems
Task 1, p. 26	Problems 3–12
Task 2, p. 27	Problems 3–12

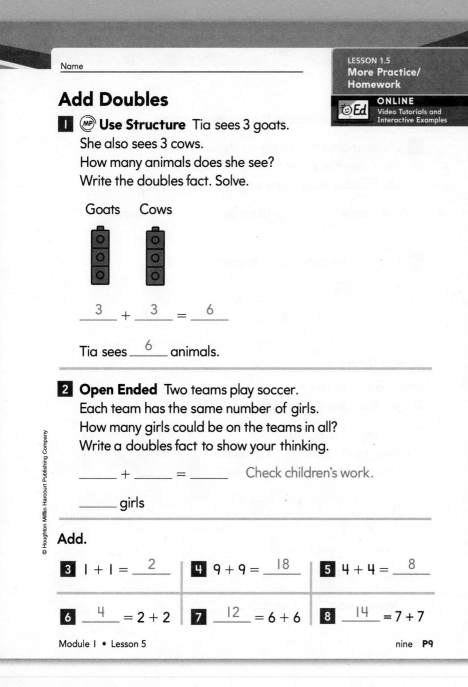

Name _____

LESSON 1.5
More Practice/ Homework

ONLINE
Video Tutorials and
Interactive Examples

Add Doubles

1 (MP) **Use Structure** Tia sees 3 goats.
She also sees 3 cows.
How many animals does she see?
Write the doubles fact. Solve.

Goats   Cows

___3___ + ___3___ = ___6___

Tia sees ___6___ animals.

2 **Open Ended** Two teams play soccer.
Each team has the same number of girls.
How many girls could be on the teams in all?
Write a doubles fact to show your thinking.

_____ + _____ = _____   Check children's work.

_____ girls

Add.

3 1 + 1 = ___2___	**4** 9 + 9 = ___18___	**5** 4 + 4 = ___8___
6 ___4___ = 2 + 2	**7** ___12___ = 6 + 6	**8** ___14___ = 7 + 7

Module 1 • Lesson 5   nine **P9**

More Practice/Homework

Add Doubles

Use More Practice/Homework pages to provide children with additional practice applying the concepts and skills presented in the lesson.

■ **Problem 1 • Use Structure** Children use a visual model to help write a doubles fact and solve a word problem.

■ **Problem 2 • Open Ended** Children write a doubles fact to represent a total made from two equal groups.

■ **Problems 3–8** Children find the sums of doubles facts.

Assignment Guide

Reference the chart below for problems associated with tasks. In a 2-day lesson, reference the chart to assign daily homework.

Learn Together Tasks	**More Practice/Homework Problems**
Task 1, p. 26	Problems 1–10
Task 2, p. 27	Problems 1–10

Test Prep

The Test Prep items provided assess understanding of doubles.

Additional Test Prep opportunities are available online and in *Getting Ready for High Stakes Assessments.*

Spiral Review

The spiral review problems will help determine if children have retained information taught in the past. Here, children will need to demonstrate the ability to make a ten to add. **(1.4)**

Test Prep

Fill in the bubble next to the correct answer.

9 Kaden makes 8 greeting cards on Tuesday. He makes the same number of cards on Wednesday. How many cards does he make?

○ 4 cards   ○ 14 cards   ● 16 cards

---

10 Which is the sum of the doubles fact?

$5 + 5 =$ ▪

○ 8   ● 10   ○ 12

Spiral Review

Make a ten to solve.
Draw ● to show your thinking.

11 Tommy eats 9 grapes. Then he eats another 3 grapes. How many grapes does he eat?

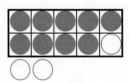

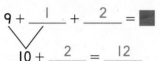

$9 + \underline{} + \underline{} = $ ▪

$10 + \underline{} = \underline{}$

So, $9 + 3 = \underline{}$.

Tommy eats $\underline{}$ grapes.

1.6 Use Known Sums to Add

LESSON FOCUS AND COHERENCE

■ Major ☐ Supporting ○ Additional

Mathematics Standards
■ Add and subtract within 20, demonstrating fluency for addition and subtraction within 10. Use strategies such as counting on; making ten (e.g., $8 + 6 = 8 + 2 + 4 = 10 + 4 = 14$); decomposing a number leading to a ten (e.g., $13 - 4 = 13 - 3 - 1 = 10 - 1 = 9$); using the relationship between addition and subtraction (e.g., knowing that $8 + 4 = 12$, one knows $12 - 8 = 4$); and creating equivalent but easier or known sums (e.g., adding $6 + 7$ by creating the known equivalent $6 + 6 + 1 = 12 + 1 = 13$).

Mathematical Practices and Processes (MP)
• Reason abstractly and quantitatively.
• Construct viable arguments and critique the reasoning of others.
• Look for and express regularity in repeated reasoning.

I Can Objective
I can use doubles facts to help add other facts.

Learning Objective
Use doubles facts to solve other addition facts.

Language Objectives
• Explain what a doubles fact is.
• Describe how to use doubles facts to solve other facts.

Lesson Materials: connecting cubes, two-color counters, crayons, pencils, MathBoard

Mathematical Progressions

Prior Learning	Current Development	Future Connections
Children: • solved addition word problems within 10. **(GrK, 11.3)** • represented addition within 10 using objects, drawings, and equations. **(GrK, 11.3, 11.5, 12.1, and 12.3)**	**Children:** • use known doubles facts to find the sum of other addition facts. • use concrete objects, drawings, and equations to show how doubles facts can be used to find the sum of other addition facts.	**Children:** • will use known doubles facts to find the sums of other addition facts, including sums that are 1 less. **(Gr2, 1.1)** • will use mental strategies to fluently add within 20. **(Gr2, 1.2)** • will know all sums of two one-digit numbers by memory. **(Gr2, 1.2)**

PROFESSIONAL LEARNING

About the Math
As children work throughout Grade 1 to apply strategies to solve addition facts, it will help greatly to be able to quickly solve any fact that is 1 more than a known doubles fact. In this lesson, children use known doubles facts to find the sum of a fact in which one of the addends is 1 greater. For example, if children know that $4 + 4 = 8$, they also know that the sum of $4 + 5$ is 1 greater than 8. Although the terms are not used in this lesson, some children may know this strategy as *doubles plus 1* or *near doubles*.

Similarly, this technique will help children find the sum of any fact that is 1 more than any other known fact. For example, if a child already knows that $2 + 6 = 8$, this technique will help them know that $2 + 7 = 9$.

ACTIVATE PRIOR KNOWLEDGE • Doubles Facts

Use these activities to quickly assess and activate prior knowledge as needed.

Number Talk

Look at the two strings of beads.
First color some of the beads on the top string.
Then color the same number of beads on the bottom string.
Write an equation to show how many beads you colored in all.

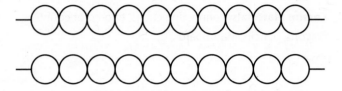

Allow children time to work out the problem above on their own. They may color any number of beads they choose, but they must color the same number on both the top string and bottom string. Children may show their thinking using paper and pencil or on their MathBoards.

Have volunteers share their work with the class as you write their equations on the board. Then ask children to tell what is similar about the equations on the board. For example, children may point out that the two numbers added together are the same in each equation or that the equations are all doubles facts.

Make Connections

Based on children's responses to the Math Routine, choose one of the following:

1 Project the Interactive Reteach, Grade 1, Lesson 1.5.

2 Complete the Prerequisite Skills Activity:

Write $6 + 6$ on the board. Ask children to tell you what is special about this fact. Possible answer: It is a double. Ask children whether they know what the sum is. 12

If children do not have the fact memorized, invite them to use addition strategies to find the sum. If no one brings it up, suggest making a ten. Have children represent the strategy using counters and ten frames.

SHARPEN SKILLS

If time permits, use this on-level activity to build fluency and practice basic skills.

Vocabulary Review

Objective: Build vocabulary fluency.

Have children answer the following math riddles:

I am an addition fact. The numbers added together are the same. What kind of fact am I? doubles fact

I am a symbol that you use to add two numbers. What symbol am I? plus (+)

I am a symbol that you use to show that two amounts are the same, or have the same value.
What symbol am I? is equal to (=)

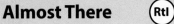

Small-Group Options

Use these teacher-guided activities with pulled small groups at the teacher table.

On Track

Have children choose a number from 1 to 9 and explain how to write a doubles fact by adding that number to itself. Then have them add 1 to one of the numbers and explain how to use the original doubles fact to find the sum of the new fact. Repeat the activity with other numbers.

Almost There (RtI)

Materials: connecting cubes

Use this Tabletop Flipchart Mini-Lesson to guide children as they use what they know about doubles facts to find the sum of other addition facts. They may use connecting cubes and equations to justify their reasoning.

Tabletop Flipchart:
Lesson 1.6

Mini-Lesson

Ready for More

Write 9 + 9 on the board and ask children to name the sum. 18

Ask: How can you use 9 + 9 = 18 to help find the sum of 9 + 8? Possible answer: The sum of 9 + 8 will be 1 less than the sum of 9 + 9. So, 9 + 8 = 17.

Then invite children to explain how they can use the fact 7 + 7 = 14 to help find the sum of 6 + 7.

Math Center Options

Use these student self-directed activities at centers or stations.

Key: ● Print Resources ● Online Resources

On Track

- ●● More Practice/Homework 1.6
- ● Poggles MX: Addition and Subtraction, Level 21, Unknown Partners Through 10

Almost There

- ● Reteach 1.6
- ● Interactive Reteach 1.6

Ready for More

- ● Challenge 1.6
- ● Interactive Challenge 1.6

ONLINE Ed View data-driven grouping recommendations and assign differentiation resources.

During the *Spark Your Learning,* listen and watch for strategies students use. See samples of student work on this page.

Use a Doubles Fact
Strategy 1

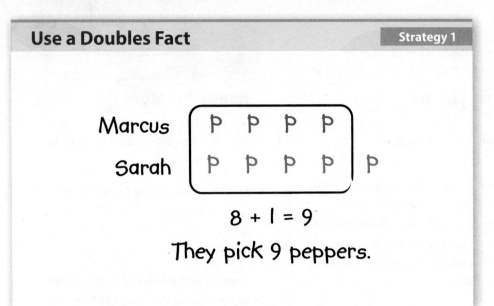

If children . . . use the doubles fact 4 + 4 = 8 to help them get the answer, they are demonstrating exemplary understanding of using doubles to find the sum of other facts. (It is not expected that children will know how to do this yet.)

Have these children . . . share and explain how they solved the problem. **Ask:**

Q How did you find how many peppers they picked?

Q How can you tell when an addition fact is 1 greater than a double?

Count Each One
Strategy 2

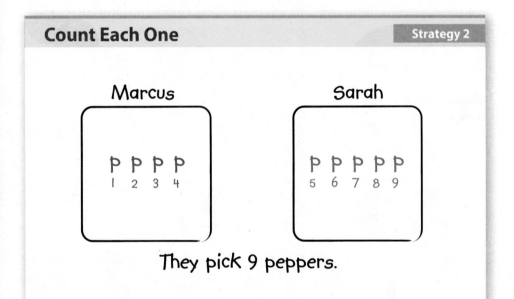

If children . . . count each pepper, they have successfully completed the activity but may benefit from understanding how a doubles fact can help them solve the problem.

Activate prior knowledge . . . by encouraging them to think about doubles facts. **Ask:**

Q What doubles facts do you know that are close to 4 + 5?

Q Circle Marcus's 4 peppers. Circle 4 of Sarah's peppers. Do you see a doubles fact? Explain.

COMMON ERROR: Subtracts

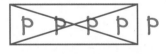

If children . . . subtract instead of add, they may have difficulty understanding the problem.

Then intervene . . . by asking children to interpret their visual models. **Ask:**

Q What does your drawing show?

Q Does it make sense to add or to subtract to solve the problem? Explain.

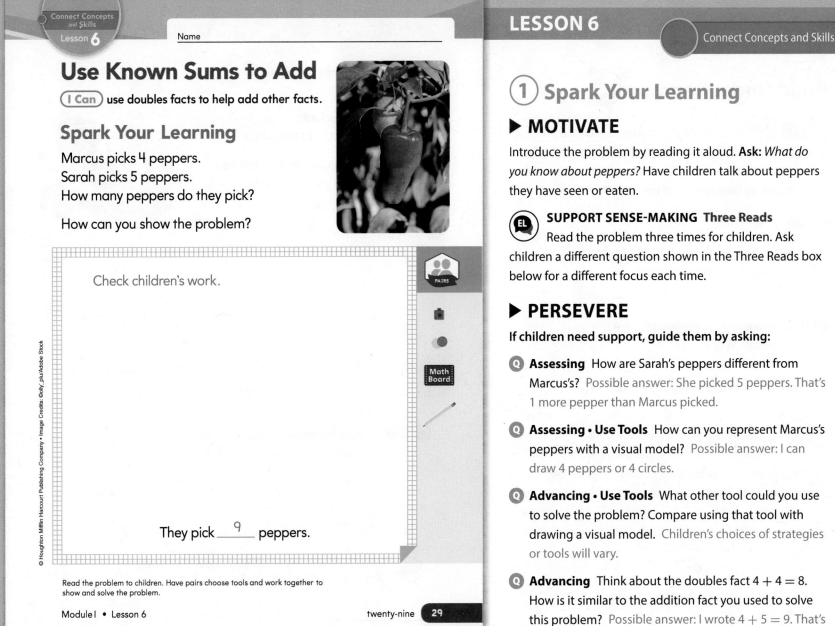

Use Known Sums to Add

(I Can) use doubles facts to help add other facts.

Spark Your Learning

Marcus picks 4 peppers.
Sarah picks 5 peppers.
How many peppers do they pick?

How can you show the problem?

Check children's work.

They pick ___9___ peppers.

Read the problem to children. Have pairs choose tools and work together to show and solve the problem.

Module 1 • Lesson 6

twenty-nine **29**

① Spark Your Learning

▶ MOTIVATE

Introduce the problem by reading it aloud. **Ask:** *What do you know about peppers?* Have children talk about peppers they have seen or eaten.

EL **SUPPORT SENSE-MAKING Three Reads**
Read the problem three times for children. Ask children a different question shown in the Three Reads box below for a different focus each time.

▶ PERSEVERE

If children need support, guide them by asking:

Q **Assessing** How are Sarah's peppers different from Marcus's? Possible answer: She picked 5 peppers. That's 1 more pepper than Marcus picked.

Q **Assessing • Use Tools** How can you represent Marcus's peppers with a visual model? Possible answer: I can draw 4 peppers or 4 circles.

Q **Advancing • Use Tools** What other tool could you use to solve the problem? Compare using that tool with drawing a visual model. Children's choices of strategies or tools will vary.

Q **Advancing** Think about the doubles fact $4 + 4 = 8$. How is it similar to the addition fact you used to solve this problem? Possible answer: I wrote $4 + 5 = 9$. That's almost the same as $4 + 4 = 8$, except one of the numbers I add is 1 greater, and the sum is 1 greater.

Turn and Talk Amy uses counters to represent an addition fact. If she adds 1 more counter, how will that change the addition fact? Possible answer: The sum will be 1 more.

EL **OPTIMIZE OUTPUT**
Stronger and Clearer

Have children share their Turn and Talk reponses. Remind children to ask questions of each other that focus on how adding 1 counter changes an addition fact. Then, have children refine their answers.

▶ BUILD SHARED UNDERSTANDING

Select children who have used various strategies and tools to share with the class how they solved the problem. Have children discuss why they chose a specific strategy or tool.

EL **SUPPORT SENSE-MAKING • Three Reads**

Read the problem stem three times and prompt the children with a different question each time.

1 What is the problem about?
Children pick some peppers.

2 What do each of the numbers describe?
Marcus picks 4 peppers. Sarah picks 5 peppers.

3 What math questions could you ask about the problem?
Possible questions: What equation models the problem? How many peppers do they pick?

② Learn Together

Build Understanding

Task 1 (MP) **Reason** As children use doubles to solve other facts, encourage them to think both quantitatively (with the use of objects or pictures to represent the facts) and abstractly (with the use of equations only).

Sample Guided Discussion:

Q **How can you show the two addition facts?** Possible answer: I can use connecting cubes to show the numbers I add.

Q **How is your representation of 3 + 4 like your representation of 3 + 3?** Possible answer: They are the same, except I use 1 more cube for 3 + 4.

Q **What addition fact models the problem?** 3 + 4 = 7

> **Turn and Talk** If children are not sure how to answer the question, encourage them to think about how their two concrete or visual models are similar and how they are different. Possible answer: My concrete model for 3 + 4 has 1 more connecting cube than my concrete model for 3 + 3. So, the sum of 3 + 4 is 1 more than the sum of 3 + 3.

Build Understanding

Ken draws 3 pictures.
Isabel draws 4 pictures.
How many pictures do they draw?

A How can you use the doubles fact 3 + 3 to help you find the sum of 3 + 4?

Possible work shown.

3 + 3 = __6__   3 + 4 = __7__

B So, they draw __7__ pictures.

C Explain how knowing the doubles fact 3 + 3 helps you find the sum of 3 + 4.

Possible answer: 4 is 1 more than 3, so the sum of 3 + 4 is 1 more than the sum of 3 + 3.

> **Turn and Talk** How do you know that the sum of 3 + 4 is 1 more than the sum of 3 + 3?
> See possible answer at the left.

30 thirty

LEVELED QUESTIONS

Depth of Knowledge (DOK)	Leveled Questions	What Does This Tell You?
Level 1 **Recall**	What doubles fact did you use to help solve 3 + 4? 3 + 3 = 4	Children's answers to this question will demonstrate whether they can identify when a doubles fact is used to find the sum of another addition fact.
Level 2 **Basic Application of Skills & Concepts**	What if Ken draws 4 pictures and then Isabel draws 5? Can you use doubles to solve that? Explain. yes; Possible answer: 4 + 4 = 8, so 4 + 5 is 1 more, or 9.	Children's answers to this question will demonstrate whether they can use doubles to solve an addition fact with a sum that is 1 greater.
Level 3 **Strategic Thinking & Complex Reasoning**	What is an example of a fact that you could solve using doubles? Explain. Answers may include any fact that is 1 more than a doubles fact. Also accept other answers if children can explain their reasoning.	Children's answers to this question will demonstrate whether they can explain how doubles can be used to solve other facts.

Step It Out

1 Use a doubles fact to add 5 + 6.

A 5 + 5 = __10__

THINK: 5 + 6 is 1 more.

So, 5 + 6 = __11__.

5 + 6

2 Use a doubles fact to add 6 + 5.

A 5 + 5 = __10__

THINK: 6 + 5 is 1 more.

So, 6 + 5 = __11__.

6 + 5

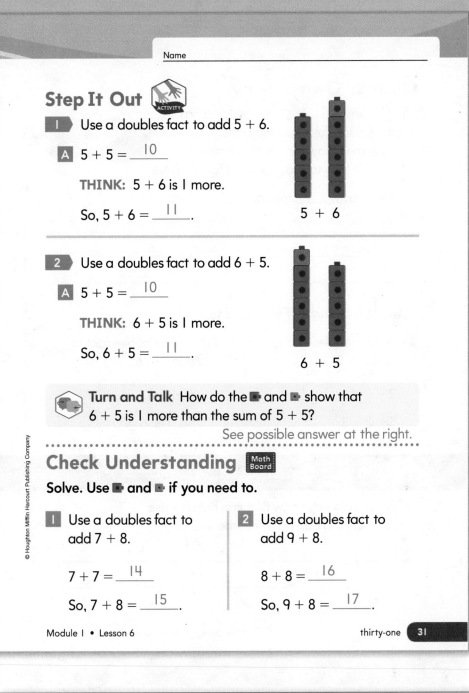

Turn and Talk How do the ■ and ■ show that 6 + 5 is 1 more than the sum of 5 + 5?

See possible answer at the right.

Check Understanding [Math Board]

Solve. Use ■ and ■ if you need to.

1 Use a doubles fact to add 7 + 8.

7 + 7 = __14__

So, 7 + 8 = __15__.

2 Use a doubles fact to add 9 + 8.

8 + 8 = __16__

So, 9 + 8 = __17__.

Step It Out

Tasks 2 and 3 (MP) **Use Repeated Reasoning** Encourage children to look for patterns and make generalizations as they use doubles to solve other addition facts.

Sample Guided Discussion:

Q **Why is 5 + 6 one more than 5 + 5?** Possible answer: The concrete model of 5 + 6 is exactly the same as 5 + 5, but with 1 more cube. So, the sum is 1 more.

Q **Why can you use the doubles fact 5 + 5 to solve either 5 + 6 or 6 + 5?** Possible answer: 5 + 6 and 6 + 5 are both like 5 + 5, but with 1 more.

Q **Think about the doubles fact 4 + 4 = 8. What addition facts have a sum that is 1 more?** Possible answer: 4 + 5 and 5 + 4

Turn and Talk Encourage children to look again at the visual model before answering.

Possible answer: The blue cubes show the doubles fact 5 + 5 = 10. When I add 1 more red cube, the sum is 1 more, too.

data
checkpoint

---

③ Check Understanding

Formative Assessment

Use formative assessment to determine if your children are successful with this lesson's learning objective.

Children who successfully complete the Check Understanding can continue to the On Your Own practice.

For children who miss 1 problem or more, work in a pulled small group with the Tabletop Flipchart Mini-Lesson.

ONLINE

Assign the Digital Check Understanding to determine
- success with the learning objective
- items to review
- grouping and differentiation resources

④ Differentiation Options

Differentiate instruction for all children using small-group mini-lessons and math center activities on page 29C.

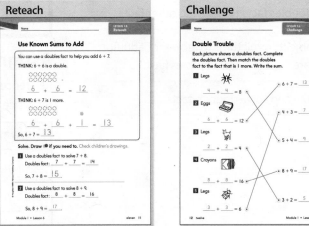

On Your Own

- **Problem 3 · Construct Arguments** Children solve a problem with a fact that is 1 away from a doubles fact. Then children provide an explanation for their work.

- **Problems 4 and 5** Children use doubles facts and connecting cubes to find sums of other facts.

(EL) OPTIMIZE OUTPUT
Critique, Correct, and Clarify

Have children share their responses to Problem 3. Encourage children to question the thinking of their partner. Discuss how they approached the problem. Children should refine their responses after their discussions with a partner.

(5) Wrap-Up

Summarize learning with your class. Consider using the Exit Ticket, Put It in Writing, or I Can scale.

Exit Ticket 🔘

Use doubles to solve. What is the sum of $9 + 8$? 17

Put It in Writing 📝

Explain how to use doubles to find the sum of $8 + 7$.

I Can 🔘

The scale below can help you and your students understand their progress on a learning goal.

4	I can show how to use a doubles fact to find the sum of another addition fact and explain when it makes sense to use the strategy.
3	I can use doubles facts to help add other facts.
2	I can use objects or pictures to represent addition facts that are 1 more than a doubles fact.
1	I can identify and solve doubles facts.

On Your Own

3 **(MP) Construct Arguments** Ming has 4 toy cars. Luke has 3 toy cars. How many toy cars do they have? Explain how to use a doubles fact to solve.

They have ___7___ toy cars.

Possible answer: 4 is 1 more than 3, so the sum of $4 + 3$
is 1 more than the sum of $3 + 3$. $3 + 3 = 6$, so $4 + 3 = 7$.

Solve. Use ▪ and ▪ if you need to.

4 Use a doubles fact to add $2 + 3$.

$2 + 2 = $ ___4___

So, $2 + 3 = $ ___5___ .

5 Use a doubles fact to add $7 + 6$.

$6 + 6 = $ ___12___

So, $7 + 6 = $ ___13___ .

💠 I'm in a Learning Mindset!

What do I already know that can help me use doubles facts to add other numbers?

_____

_____

_____

Learning Mindset

mindset works

Try Again   Collects and Tries Multiple Strategies

Provide children with the opportunity to reflect on all of the strategies they used in this module. Discuss specific ways in which they adapted known strategies to use doubles facts to add other numbers. *The more strategies you know, the more times you will be able to try to solve a problem. If you can try to solve a problem five different ways, you are more likely to be successful than if you can try to solve a problem only two different ways.*

Assignment Guide

Reference the chart below for problems associated with tasks. In a 2-day lesson, reference the chart to assign daily homework.

Learn Together Tasks	On Your Own Problems
Task 1, p. 30	Problem 3
Task 2, p. 31	Problem 4
Task 3, p. 31	Problem 5

Name _____

Use Known Sums to Add

LESSON 1.6
**More Practice/
Homework**

 **ONLINE**
Video Tutorials and
Interactive Examples

1 Use a doubles fact to add 4 + 5.

$4 + 4 =$ ___8___

So, $4 + 5 =$ ___9___.

2 Use a doubles fact to add 6 + 5.

$5 + 5 =$ ___10___

So, $6 + 5 =$ ___11___.

3 **Math on the Spot** Brianna has 8 toy ducks.
Ian has the same number of toy ducks
and a toy fish. How many toys do
Brianna and Ian have?

___17___ toys

4 (MP) **Construct Arguments** Ted has 7 shells.
Then he finds 8 more shells.
How many shells does he have now?
Explain how to use a doubles fact to solve.

Ted has ___15___ shells now.

Possible answer: 8 is 1 more than 7, so the sum of 7 + 8 is

1 more than the sum of 7 + 7. 7 + 7 = 14, so 7 + 8 = 15.

Module 1 • Lesson 6   eleven **P11**

Assign the Digital More Practice/
Homework for
• built-in student supports
• Actionable Item Reports
• Standards Analysis Reports

More Practice/Homework

Use Known Sums to Add

Use More Practice/Homework pages to provide children
with additional practice applying the concepts and skills
presented in the lesson.

- **Problems 1 and 2** Children use a known doubles fact to
  find the sum of a fact that is 1 more.

- **Problem 4 • Construct Arguments** Children explain
  how to use a doubles fact to find the sum of another fact.

Math on the Spot

Encourage children to complete
Problem 3 and then review their
work with a family member or
friend by watching the *Math on
the Spot* video.

Assignment Guide

Reference the chart below for problems associated with tasks. In a 2-day lesson,
reference the chart to assign daily homework.

Learn Together Tasks	More Practice/Homework Problems
Task 1, p. 30	Problems 3, 4, and 5
Task 2, p. 31	Problems 1 and 6
Task 3, p. 31	Problems 2 and 7

Lesson 1.6   32A

Test Prep

The Test Prep items provided assess understanding of using doubles to solve other addition facts.

Additional Test Prep opportunities are available online and in *Getting Ready for High Stakes Assessments.*

Spiral Review

The spiral review problems will help determine if children have retained information taught in the past. Here, children will need to demonstrate the ability to add doubles. **(1.5)**

Test Prep

Fill in the bubble next to the correct answer.

5 Tyler has 6 toy dogs.
Maya has 7 toy dogs.
How many toy dogs do they have?

○ 11 toy dogs   ● 13 toy dogs   ○ 15 toy dogs

6 Use a doubles fact to add. Which is the sum?

$3 + 4 = $ ■

● 7   ○ 8   ○ 9

7 Use a doubles fact to add. Which is the sum?

$8 + 7 = $ ■

○ 13   ● 15   ○ 17

Spiral Review

Write the doubles fact. Solve.

8 James counts 4 people in the deli.
Then 4 more people walk in.
How many people are in the deli now?

__4__ + __4__ = __8__   __8__ people

Add.

9 $6 + 6 = $ __12__   **10** $5 + 5 = $ __10__   **11** __18__ $= 9 + 9$

1.7 Choose a Strategy to Add

LESSON FOCUS AND COHERENCE

■ Major ☐ Supporting ○ Additional

Mathematics Standards

■ Use addition and subtraction within 20 to solve word problems involving situations of adding to, taking from, putting together, taking apart, and comparing, with unknowns in all positions, e.g., by using objects, drawings, and equations with a symbol for the unknown number to represent the problem.

■ Add and subtract within 20, demonstrating fluency for addition and subtraction within 10. Use strategies such as counting on; making ten (e.g., $8 + 6 = 8 + 2 + 4 = 10 + 4 = 14$); decomposing a number leading to a ten (e.g., $13 - 4 = 13 - 3 - 1 = 10 - 1 = 9$); using the relationship between addition and subtraction (e.g., knowing that $8 + 4 = 12$, one knows $12 - 8 = 4$); and creating equivalent but easier or known sums (e.g., adding $6 + 7$ by creating the known equivalent $6 + 6 + 1 = 12 + 1 = 13$).

Mathematical Practices and Processes (MP)

- Reason abstractly and quantitatively.
- Construct viable arguments and critique the reasoning of others.

I Can Objective

I can choose a strategy to solve an addition problem.

Learning Objective

Apply strategies such as making a ten, counting on, and using doubles to solve addition word problems.

Language Objective

- Explain how to decide which addition strategy to use to solve a problem.

Lesson Materials: connecting cubes, two-color counters

Mathematical Progressions

Prior Learning	Current Development	Future Connections
Children: • solved addition word problems within 10. **(GrK, 11.3)** • represented addition within 10 using objects, drawings, and equations. **(GrK, 11.3, 11.5, 12.1, and 12.3)**	**Children:** • use strategies to add within 20, including counting on, making a ten, and using known doubles facts. • solve addition word problems within 20, using objects, drawings, and equations.	**Children:** • will use mental strategies to fluently add within 20. **(Gr2, 1.2)** • will use addition within 100 to solve one- and two-step word problems. **(Gr2, 15.1 and 15.3)**

PROFESSIONAL LEARNING

About the Math

Why Teach This? One of the main achievements of Grade 1 is being able to apply strategies to add within 20. In this lesson, children learn to choose an addition strategy that is appropriate and efficient for specific problems and quantities. The understanding of how to choose and use a strategy to add will be the foundation for children's work with addition throughout Grade 1.

WARM-UP OPTIONS

ACTIVATE PRIOR KNOWLEDGE • Count On

Use these activities to quickly assess and activate prior knowledge as needed.

Math Routine

Number Talk

How can you use the number line to show $3 + 6$?

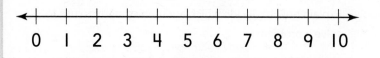

Display the problem above and have children solve it on their own. Provide number lines or have children draw number lines on their MathBoards to illustrate their thinking.

Invite volunteers to share their answers with the class. Encourage a variety of responses, such as starting at 3 and counting 6 more, starting at 6 and counting on 3, or circling 3 numbers one color and 6 numbers another color.

Ask: Which stategy do you like the best? Which stategy do you think is the fastest? Explain.

Make Connections

Based on children's responses to the Math Routine, choose one of the following:

1 Project the Interactive Reteach, Grade 1, Lesson 1.2.

2 Complete the Prerequisite Skills Activity:

Draw a number line from 0–10 on the board. Invite children to explain how to count on to find the sum of $7 + 2$. Possible answer: Start at 7. Make 2 jumps. I land on 9. So, $7 + 2 = 9$.

Then invite children to show how to use counters or connecting cubes to count on to find the sum of $3 + 8$.

If children continue to struggle, use Tier 2 Skill 13.

SHARPEN SKILLS

If time permits, use this on-level activity to to build fluency and practice basic skills.

Fluency—Addition and Subtraction Within 5

Objective: Fluently add and subtract within 5.

Materials: Fluency Maintenance: Addition and Subtraction (Differentiated Instruction Blackline Masters)

Have children find each sum or difference.

$3 + 2 = \underline{5}$ $5 - 4 = \underline{1}$

$4 - 2 = \underline{2}$ $1 - 0 = \underline{1}$

$1 + 3 = \underline{4}$ $2 + 1 = \underline{3}$

Children can then complete the Fluency Maintenance worksheet to practice addition and subtraction within 5.

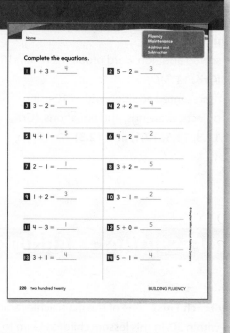

Small-Group Options

Use these teacher-guided activities with pulled small groups at the teacher table.

On Track

Materials: per pair: Number Cards 0–9 (Teacher Resource Masters), Ten Frames (Teacher Resource Masters), Number Line 0–12 (Teacher Resource Masters), two-color counters, connecting cubes

Have partners simultaneously take two Number Cards and place the cards in front of themselves. Then have children use any desired manipulatives to add the numbers, using whatever strategy seems best to them. When they finish, invite each pair to compare their work with the work of other pairs.

Repeat the activity several times, as time allows.

Almost There (RtI)

Materials: connecting cubes, Ten Frames (Teacher Resource Masters), two-color counters

Use this Tabletop Flipchart Mini-Lesson to guide children as they use two different strategies to solve an addition word problem and use concrete objects, drawings, and equations to justify their reasoning.

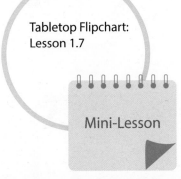

Tabletop Flipchart:
Lesson 1.7

Mini-Lesson

Ready for More

Materials: per pair: Number Cards 0–9 (Teacher Resource Masters), Sign Cards + and – (Teacher Resource Masters)

Have each partner use two Number Cards and one Sign Card to make an addition or subtraction problem. Children with the minus symbol should be careful to put the card with the greater number first. Partners then explain to each other how to solve, using whichever strategy they prefer.

Repeat the activity several times, as time allows.

Math Center Options

Use these student self-directed activities at centers or stations.   **Key:** ● Print Resources ● Online Resources

On Track

- ●● Additional Practice 1.7
- ●● More Practice/Homework 1.7
- ● Fluency Maintenance: Addition and Subtraction
- ● My Learning Summary
- ● Poggles MX: Addition and Subtraction, Level 29, Add Through 20

Almost There

- ● Reteach 1.7
- ● Interactive Reteach 1.7
- ●● RtI Tier 2 Skill 13: Count On

Ready for More

- ● Challenge 1.7
- ● Interactive Challenge 1.7

Unit Project Check children's progress by asking them to explain an addition strategy that can be used to find the total number of sounds they make.

ONLINE ☺Ed   View data-driven grouping recommendations and assign differentiation resources.

What to Watch For

During the Step It Out activity, listen and watch for possible errors students might make. See samples of student work on this page.

Use the *Then intervene . . .* suggestions to help students understand their error and make sense of the mathematics.

COMMON ERROR: Makes 10 Without Decomposing the Other Addend

Make a ten to add 8 + 7.

$8 + 2 + 7 = \blacksquare$

$10 + 7 = 17$

So, $8 + 7 = 17$.

Watch for . . . children in Task 1 who add 2 to 8 to make 10, but forget to break apart the 7 into 2 and 5.

Then intervene . . . by having children make a concrete model using counters and a ten frame so that they can see how many they have left to add. **Ask:**

Q How many did you add to 8 to get to ten?

Q So, how many more do you have left to add?

Q How can you use the *make a ten* strategy to solve this problem?

COMMON ERROR: 1 Less Than the Double

Use a doubles fact to help add 8 + 7.

$7 + 7 = 14$

So, $8 + 7 = 13$.

Watch for . . . children in Task 2 who subtract 1 from the sum of $7 + 7$ instead of adding 1.

Then intervene . . . by asking them how they know whether the sum of $8 + 7$ is 1 more than the sum of $7 + 7$ or 1 less than the sum of $7 + 7$. **Ask:**

Q How do you know whether to add 1 or subtract 1 from the doubles fact to find your answer?

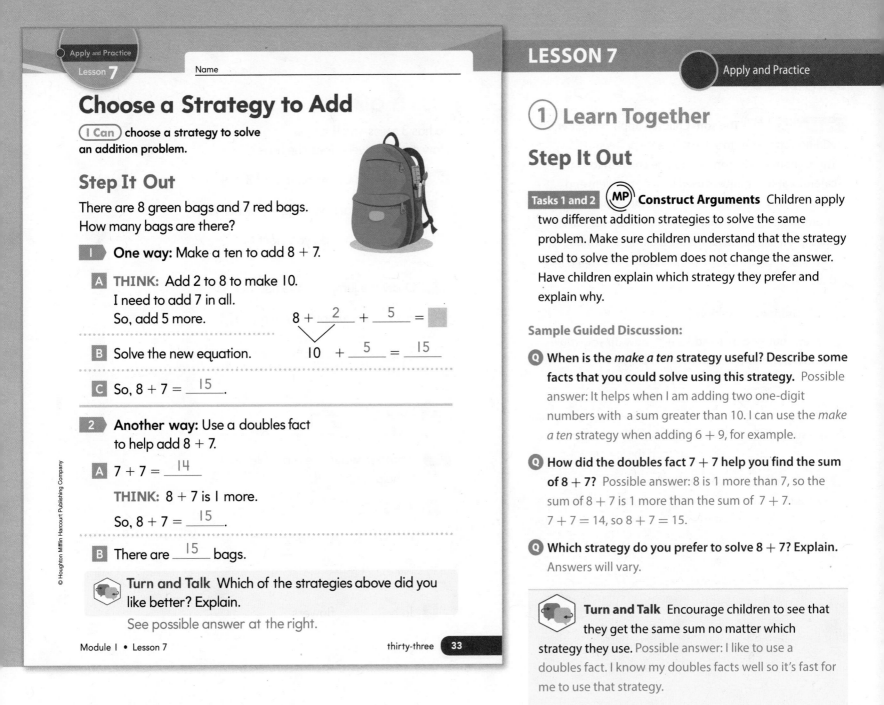

Choose a Strategy to Add

(I Can) choose a strategy to solve an addition problem.

Step It Out

There are 8 green bags and 7 red bags. How many bags are there?

1 **One way:** Make a ten to add $8 + 7$.

A THINK: Add 2 to 8 to make 10.
I need to add 7 in all.
So, add 5 more.

$8 + \underline{2} + \underline{5} = \blacksquare$

B Solve the new equation.

$10 + \underline{5} = \underline{15}$

C So, $8 + 7 = \underline{15}$.

2 **Another way:** Use a doubles fact to help add $8 + 7$.

A $7 + 7 = \underline{14}$

THINK: $8 + 7$ is 1 more.

So, $8 + 7 = \underline{15}$.

B There are $\underline{15}$ bags.

Turn and Talk Which of the strategies above did you like better? Explain.

See possible answer at the right.

© Houghton Mifflin Harcourt Publishing Company

---

① Learn Together

Step It Out

Tasks 1 and 2 **(MP)** **Construct Arguments** Children apply two different addition strategies to solve the same problem. Make sure children understand that the strategy used to solve the problem does not change the answer. Have children explain which strategy they prefer and explain why.

Sample Guided Discussion:

Q When is the *make a ten* strategy useful? Describe some facts that you could solve using this strategy. Possible answer: It helps when I am adding two one-digit numbers with a sum greater than 10. I can use the *make a ten* strategy when adding $6 + 9$, for example.

Q How did the doubles fact $7 + 7$ help you find the sum of $8 + 7$? Possible answer: 8 is 1 more than 7, so the sum of $8 + 7$ is 1 more than the sum of $7 + 7$. $7 + 7 = 14$, so $8 + 7 = 15$.

Q Which strategy do you prefer to solve $8 + 7$? Explain. Answers will vary.

Turn and Talk Encourage children to see that they get the same sum no matter which strategy they use. Possible answer: I like to use a doubles fact. I know my doubles facts well so it's fast for me to use that strategy.

LEVELED QUESTIONS

Depth of Knowledge (DOK)	Leveled Questions	What Does This Tell You?
Level 1 **Recall**	If there are 3 green bags and 8 red bags, which addition strategy can you use to find how many bags there are? Possible answers: make a ten; count on	Children's answers to this question will demonstrate whether they can identify an addition strategy that can be used to solve a problem.
Level 2 **Basic Application of Skills & Concepts**	If you use different strategies to solve the same addition problem, will you get different answers? Explain. no; Possible answer: The answer is always the same no matter which strategy I use to find the answer.	Children's answers to this question will demonstrate whether they understand that the addition strategy used does not affect the answer.
Level 3 **Strategic Thinking & Complex Reasoning**	Does it make sense to count on to add $8 + 7$? Explain. Possible answer: No. Counting on works best when I'm adding 1, 2, or 3. It would take too long to count on 7 or to count on 8.	Children's answers to this question will demonstrate whether they can explain why an addition strategy is or is not appropriate to solve a problem.

Step It Out

Tasks 3 and 4 (MP) **Reason** Children apply two different addition strategies to solve the same problem. Throughout this lesson, encourage children to look carefully at the numbers used in each problem and consider why certain addition strategies may not be appropriate for some math situations. For example, it does not make sense to use the *make a ten* strategy to solve the problem on this page because the sum is less than 10.

Sample Guided Discussion:

Q **When counting on to add 3 + 4, how do you know which number to start on?** Possible answer: I start with the greater number (4) because it's faster.

Q **How do you know that the sum of 3 + 4 is 1 more than the sum of 3 + 3?** Possible answer: 4 is 1 more than 3, so the sum of 3 + 4 is 1 more than the sum of 3 + 3.

Q **Which strategy do you prefer to solve 3 + 4? Explain.** Answers will vary. Possible answer: I like to count on using a number line. It's the fastest way for me to solve.

Step It Out

Jo has 3 roses and 4 tulips.
How many flowers does she have?

3 **One way:** Count on to add 3 + 4.

A **THINK:** Start on the greater number.

What number do you start on? __4__

B Draw the jumps on the number line.

How many jumps do you make? __3__

C So, 3 + 4 = __7__.

4 **Another way:** Use a doubles fact to help add 3 + 4.

A 3 + 3 = __6__

THINK: 3 + 4 is 1 more.

So, 3 + 4 = __7__.

B Jo has __7__ flowers.

9 dogs play. 3 dogs sleep.
How many dogs are there?

5 **One way:** Count on to add $9 + 3$.

A Start with 9. Count on 3 more.

9, _10_, _11_, _12_

B So, $9 + 3 =$ _12_.

6 **Another way:** Make a ten to add $9 + 3$.

A **THINK:** Add 1 to 9 to make 10.
I need to add 3 in all.
So, add 2 more.

$9 +$ _1_ $+$ _2_ $=$ ▨

B Solve the new equation.

$10 +$ _2_ $=$ _12_

C So, $9 + 3 =$ _12_.

D There are _12_ dogs.

Check Understanding [Math Board]

Use any strategy. Draw to show your work.

1 7 boys wear blue. 6 boys wear red.
How many boys are there?

Check children's drawings.

_13_ boys

Module 1 • Lesson 7 — thirty-five **35**

Task 5 and 6 **(MP)** **Construct Argument** Children apply two different addition strategies to solve the same problem. Encourage children to tell which strategy they prefer to solve this problem and explain their reasoning.

Sample Guided Discussion:

Q **When you count on to add $9 + 3$, why do you start with 9?** Possible answer: Starting with 3 and counting 9 more takes too long. It's faster to start with 9 and count on 3.

Q **Which strategy do you prefer when solving $9 + 3$? Why?** Answers will vary. Possible answer: I like to count on. When I add a small number like 3, I can quickly find the sum by counting on.

data checkpoint

---

② Check Understanding

Formative Assessment

Use formative assessment to determine if your children are successful with this lesson's learning objective.

Children who successfully complete the Check Understanding can continue to the On Your Own practice.

For children who missed the Check Understanding problem, work in a pulled small group with the Tabletop Flipchart Mini-Lesson.

ONLINE **Assign the Digital Check Understanding to determine**
• success with the learning objective
• items to review
• grouping and differentiation resources

③ Differentiation Options

Differentiate instruction for all children using small-group mini-lessons and math center activities on page 33C.

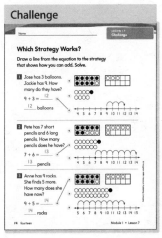

On Your Own

- **Problem 2 · Attend to Precision** Children choose a strategy to solve an addition problem. Encourage precise mathematical communication as children draw to illustrate their thinking.

- **Problem 3 · Open Ended** Children use two different strategies to solve the same addition fact.

EL **OPTIMIZE OUTPUT**
Critique, Correct, and Clarify

Have children share their responses to Problem 2. Encourage children to question the thinking of their partner and discuss how they decided which strategy would best help them solve the problem. Children should refine their responses after their discussions with a partner.

On Your Own

MP Attend to Precision Use any strategy. Draw to show your work.

2 Julian has 7 marbles.
His brother gives him 4 more.
How many marbles does Julian have now?

> Check children's drawings.

Julian has __11__ marbles.

3 **Open Ended** Use two different strategies to add.

$7 + 8 = $ __15__

Check children's work. Accept all reasonable strategies.

One Way	Another Way

© Houghton Mifflin Harcourt Publishing Company • Image Credits: ©Ivonne Wierink/Adobe Stock

36   thirty-six

Assignment Guide

Reference the chart below for problems associated with tasks. In a 2-day lesson, reference the chart to assign daily homework.

Learn Together Tasks	On Your Own Problems
Tasks 1 and 6, pp. 33 and 35	Problems 2, 3, 4, 5, 7, 8, 10, 11, 12, and 13
Tasks 2 and 4, pp. 33 and 34	Problems 3, 8, and 9
Tasks 3 and 5, pp. 34 and 35	Problems 6, 7, 13, and 14

Name _____

On Your Own

Use any strategy. Write an equation.

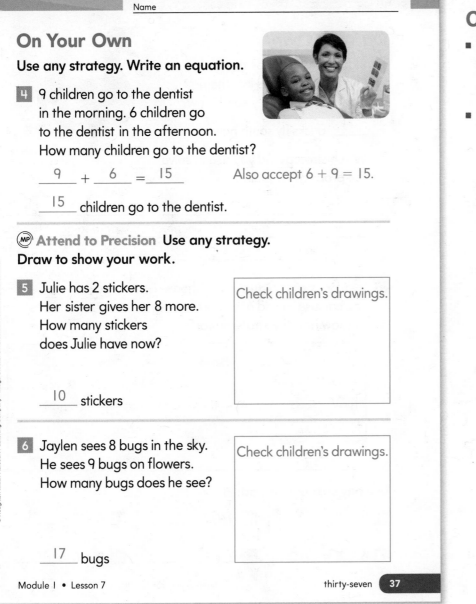

4 9 children go to the dentist in the morning. 6 children go to the dentist in the afternoon. How many children go to the dentist?

___9___ + ___6___ = ___15___   Also accept 6 + 9 = 15.

___15___ children go to the dentist.

(MP) **Attend to Precision** **Use any strategy.**
Draw to show your work.

5 Julie has 2 stickers. Her sister gives her 8 more. How many stickers does Julie have now?

Check children's drawings.

___10___ stickers

---

6 Jaylen sees 8 bugs in the sky. He sees 9 bugs on flowers. How many bugs does he see?

Check children's drawings.

___17___ bugs

© Houghton Mifflin Harcourt Publishing Company • Image Credits: ©WavebreakmediaMicro/Adobe Stock

On Your Own

■ **Problem 4 • Health and Fitness** Going to the dentist is an important part of taking care of one's teeth. A dentist might clean a person's teeth or look for cavities.

■ **Problems 5 and 6 • Attend to Precision** Children choose a strategy to solve an addition problem. Encourage precise mathematical communication as children draw to illustrate their thinking.

On Your Own

- **Problem 7 • STEM** Some ducks fly south every winter. They prefer the warmer weather there. At the end of the winter, they fly back north again.

- **Problem 8 • Construct Arguments** Children justify why a particular strategy would help them to solve a given problem.

- **Problems 9–14** Children use any strategy to solve basic addition facts.

④ Wrap-Up

Summarize learning with your class. Consider using the Exit Ticket, Put It in Writing, or I Can scale.

Exit Ticket

Show how to solve 9 + 8 in two ways.
Check children's work. Possible strategies include making a ten and using the doubles fact 8 + 8 = 16 to show that 9 + 8 = 17.

Put It in Writing

How do you decide which strategy to use to solve an addition fact?

I Can

The scale below can help you and your students understand their progress on a learning goal.

4	I can explain why I chose a strategy to solve an addition problem.
3	I can choose a strategy to solve an addition problem.
2	I can solve an addition problem using a given strategy.
1	I can count or count on to solve an addition problem.

On Your Own

7 3 ducks fly south for the winter. Then 8 more ducks join them. How many ducks fly south now?

_____11_____ ducks fly south now.

Which strategy did you use to solve the problem? Explain.

Possible answer: I counted on to add 3 + 8. I started with 8 because it is greater. Then I counted on 3 more to get 11. 8, 9, 10, 11. So, 3 + 8 = 11.

8 **(MP) Construct Arguments** Choose a strategy you can use to add 6 + 7. Draw or write to show how the strategy works.

> Accept all reasonable answers. Possible strategies include making a ten and using the doubles fact 6 + 6 to show that 6 + 7 = 13.

Use any strategy to add.

9 4 + 5 = ___9___	**10** 9 + 7 = ___16___	**11** 8 + 5 = ___13___
12 6 + 8 = ___14___	**13** 2 + 9 = ___11___	**14** 9 + 0 = ___9___

Keep Going ⏩ Practice and Homework Journal

© Houghton Mifflin Harcourt Publishing Company • Image Credits: ©abishiga/Adobe Stock

LESSON 1.7
More Practice/
Homework
ONLINE
Video Tutorials and
Interactive Examples

Name _____

Choose a Strategy to Add

1 (MP) **Construct Arguments**
Choose a strategy you can use
to add $9 + 8$. Draw or write
to show how the strategy works.

> Accept all reasonable answers.
> Possible strategies include making a ten
> and using the doubles fact $8 + 8$ to
> show that $9 + 8 = 17$.

2 **Open Ended** Write two numbers
to complete the word problem.
Then use any strategy to solve.
Check children's work.

_____ birds are in a tree.

_____ more birds fly there.

How many birds are in the tree now?

_____ birds

Use any strategy to add.

3 $4 + 7 = \underline{11}$ **4** $6 + 3 = \underline{9}$ **5** $9 + 5 = \underline{14}$

Module 1 • Lesson 7   thirteen **P13**

© Houghton Mifflin Harcourt Publishing Company

Assign the Digital More Practice/
Homework for
• built-in student supports
• Actionable Item Reports
• Standards Analysis Reports

More Practice/Homework

Choose a Strategy to Add

Use More Practice/Homework pages to provide children
with additional practice applying the concepts and skills
presented in the lesson.

- **Problem 1 • Construct Arguments** Children choose an
  addition strategy and show how that strategy works.

- **Problem 2 • Open Ended** Children complete an
  addition word problem and then use any strategy to
  solve it.

- **Problems 3–5** Children use any strategy to solve basic
  addition facts.

Additional Practice

Practice more with the Additional Practice page.

Assignment Guide

Reference the chart below for problems associated with tasks. In a 2-day lesson,
reference the chart to assign daily homework.

Learn Together Tasks	More Practice/Homework Problems
Tasks 1 and 6, pp. 33 and 35	Problems 1, 2, 3, 5, 6, and 7
Tasks 2 and 4, pp. 33 and 34	Problems 1, 2, and 7
Tasks 3 and 5, pp. 34 and 35	Problems 2 and 4

Test Prep

The Test Prep items provided assess understanding of using addition strategies to solve word problems.

Additional Test Prep opportunities are available online and in *Getting Ready for High Stakes Assessments.*

Spiral Review

The spiral review problems will help determine if children have retained information taught in the past. Here, children will need to demonstrate the ability to count on to add. **(1.2)**

Test Prep

Fill in the bubble next to the correct answer.

6 Juan has 8 blocks.
Tina has the same number of blocks.
How many blocks do they have?
Use any strategy to solve.

○ 4 blocks

○ 14 blocks

● 16 blocks

7 There are 6 red flowers
and 7 yellow flowers in a vase.
How many flowers are in the vase?
Use any strategy to solve.

○ 15 flowers   ● 13 flowers   ○ 11 flowers

Spiral Review

8 Jenny eats 7 grapes. Then she eats 2 more.
How many grapes does she eat?
Draw jumps on the number line to count on.

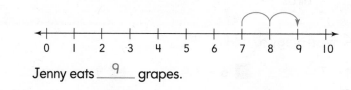

Jenny eats ___9___ grapes.

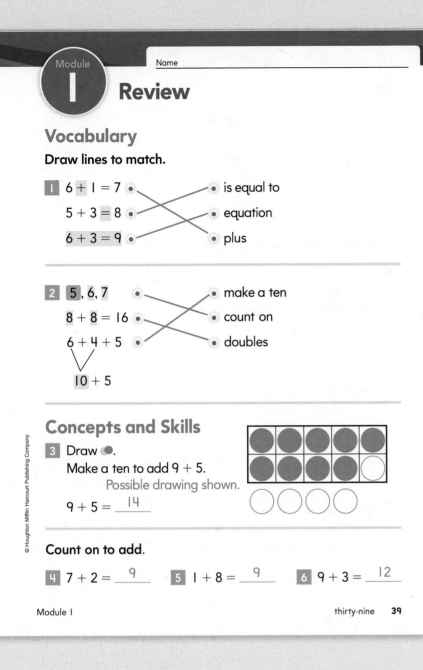

Module 1 Review

Name _____

Vocabulary

Draw lines to match.

1
- $6 + 1 = 7$ • → • is equal to
- $5 + 3 = 8$ • → • equation
- $6 + 3 = 9$ • → • plus

2
- $5, 6, 7$ • → • make a ten
- $8 + 8 = 16$ • → • count on
- $6 + 4 + 5$ • → • doubles
  - $10 + 5$

Concepts and Skills

3 Draw •.
Make a ten to add $9 + 5$.
Possible drawing shown.
$9 + 5 = \underline{14}$

Count on to add.

4 $7 + 2 = \underline{9}$ **5** $1 + 8 = \underline{9}$ **6** $9 + 3 = \underline{12}$

Module 1

thirty-nine **39**

ONLINE

Assign the Digital Module Review for
- built-in student supports
- Actionable Item Reports
- Standards Analysis Reports

MODULE 1

REVIEW

Module Review

Use the Module Review as practice and review of the module's content.

Vocabulary

Have children review the vocabulary terms for this module. Encourage children to think about the meaning of each term in their own words before completing Items 1 and 2.

Concepts and Skills

MP Use Tools Prior to assigning the Module Review, help children list the strategies or tools used throughout the module. As each is listed, guide children to think about how they might use each strategy or tool to solve a problem.

As children start the review, read Item 6. Remind children of the list of tools used in the module. Ask them to think of a strategy or a tool that could be used to solve the problem.

After children have completed the review, discuss Item 6 and ask a child to show his or her solution with the strategy or tool used. Have children who used a different tool share their solutions.

DATA-DRIVEN INSTRUCTION

Before moving on to the Module Test, use the Module Review results to intervene based on the table below.

MTSS RtI

Items	Lesson	DOK	Content Focus	Intervention
3	1.4	2	Make a ten to add.	Reteach 1.4
4 and 5	1.2	1	Count on to add.	Reteach 1.2
6	1.2	3	Count on to add.	Reteach 1.2

Module 1   **39**

© Houghton Mifflin Harcourt Publishing Company

Module Review continued

Possible Scoring Guide

Items	Points	Description
1 and 2	1	matches 1 example to the correct term
1 and 2	2	matches all examples to the correct terms
3	1	writes the correct sum or draws a correct picture
3	2	writes the correct sum and draws a correct picture
4–12	2	writes the correct sum
13–15	2	selects the correct answer
Total points possible = 30 points		

The Unit 1 Performance Task in the Assessment Guide assesses content from Modules 1–4.

Add.

7 $10 + 3 = \underline{13}$ **8** $10 + 7 = \underline{17}$

9 $6 + 7 = \underline{13}$ **10** $9 + 9 = \underline{18}$

11 $\underline{11} = 8 + 3$ **12** $\underline{14} = 6 + 8$

Fill in the bubble next to the correct answer.

13 Janelle has 8 shirts.
Then she gets 4 more shirts.
How many shirts does she have now?

○ 4 shirts   ○ 11 shirts   ● 12 shirts

14 David draws 4 pictures.
Tyshe draws 5 pictures.
How many pictures do they draw?

● 9 pictures   ○ 8 pictures   ○ 1 picture

15 Gracie paints 8 rocks.
Then she paints another 8 rocks.
How many rocks does she paint?

○ 18 rocks   ● 16 rocks   ○ 10 rocks

40 forty

DATA-DRIVEN INSTRUCTION

Before moving on to the Module Test, use the Module Review results to intervene based on the table below.

Items	Lesson	DOK	Content Focus	Intervention
7 and 8	1.3	1	Add 10 and more.	Reteach 1.3
9	1.6	2	Use doubles to solve other facts.	Reteach 1.6
10	1.5	1	Add doubles.	Reteach 1.5
11 and 12	1.7	1	Use strategies to add within 20.	Reteach 1.7
13 and 14	1.1	2	Use addition to solve a word problem.	Reteach 1.1
15	1.7	2	Choose an addition strategy to solve a word problem.	Reteach 1.7

Module Test

data
checkpoint

The Module Test is available in alternative versions in your Assessment Guide. The print versions are available in your Assessment Guide.

Assign the Digital Module Test to power actionable reports including
- proficiency by standards
- item analysis

Form A

Name _____

Module 1 • Form A
Module Test

1 There are 4 bunnies in the grass. There are 2 bunnies in the pen. Which shows counting on to find how many bunnies there are?

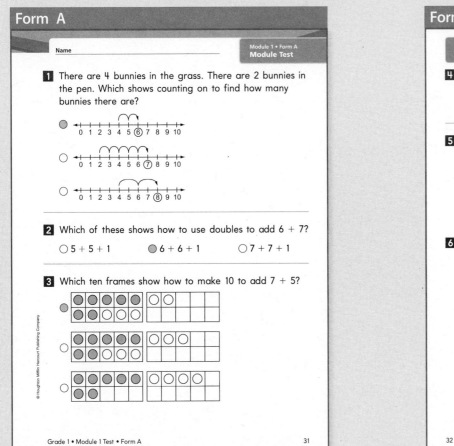

2 Which of these shows how to use doubles to add 6 + 7?

○ 5 + 5 + 1   ● 6 + 6 + 1   ○ 7 + 7 + 1

3 Which ten frames show how to make 10 to add 7 + 5?

Grade 1 • Module 1 Test • Form A   31

Form A

Module 1 • Form A
Module Test   Name _____

4 Show how to count on to add 6 + 2.

6, _7_ , _8_

5 Margo sees 9 red squirrels and 6 black squirrels. How many squirrels does Margo see?

15 _____

6 Joe washes 6 big plates. He washes 1 small plate. Write an equation to show how many plates Joe washes.
Possible answer:
_6_ + _1_ = _7_

7 Lin reads 3 pages. She reads 10 more pages. Write an equation to show how many pages Lin reads.
Possible answer:
_3_ + _10_ = _13_

8 Jeffery has 5 pennies. He gets 9 more pennies. How can Jeffery make a ten to find how many pennies he has?

Use numbers from the list to write an equation Jeffery could use.
Possible answer:
_10_ + _4_ = _14_

| 1 | 4 | 10 | 14 |

32

Form B

Name _____

Module 1 • Form B
Module Test

1 There are 7 frogs in the water. There are 2 more frogs on a log. Which shows counting on to find how many frogs there are?

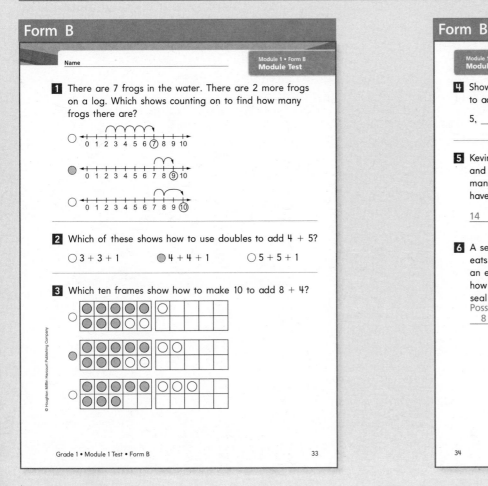

2 Which of these shows how to use doubles to add 4 + 5?

○ 3 + 3 + 1   ● 4 + 4 + 1   ○ 5 + 5 + 1

3 Which ten frames show how to make 10 to add 8 + 4?

Grade 1 • Module 1 Test • Form B   33

Form B

Module 1 • Form B
Module Test   Name _____

4 Show how to count on to add 5 + 2.

5, _6_ , _7_

5 Kevin has 9 green pears and 5 yellow pears. How many pears does Kevin have?

14 _____

6 A seal eats 8 fish. She eats 1 more fish. Write an equation to show how many fish the seal eats.
Possible answer:
_8_ + _1_ = _9_

7 Ramel has a box of 10 eggs. He has 4 more eggs in a bowl. Write an equation to show how many eggs Ramel has.
Possible answer:
_10_ + _4_ = _14_

8 Clare puts 9 books in her bag. She puts 3 more books in her bag. How can Clare make a ten to find how many books are in her bag?

Use numbers from the list to write an equation Clare could use.
Possible answer:
_10_ + _2_ = _12_

| 2 | 4 | 10 | 12 |

34